—A—
Family
REUNITED

To Hopefulness

Jeffery Tracey Sr.
Nov. 5, 2017

by

JEFFERY TRACEY SR.

PAGE PUBLISHING, INC.
New York, NY

First originally published by Page Publishing, Inc. 2017

ISBN 978-1-68348-978-8 (Paperback)
ISBN 978-1-68409-822-4 (Hard Cover)
ISBN 978-1-68348-979-5 (Digital)

Printed in the United States of America

CONTENTS

To my loving wife, Debra Tracey

In loving memory, dedicated to Mike, Bob, and Alan Tracey

CHAPTER 1

Prologue

I was born into a poor family. A family that would separate a couple of years after my birth. As an unborn child in my mother's womb, I hung in there and waited to be born in the early hours on April 2, 1952. I wasn't about to be an April fools baby. My mother and father named me Jeffery. My mother once told me I was a sickly child with severe asthma. She said I wheezed loudly when sleeping during the night. She told me I often had a cold, flu, and sometimes pneumonia. She told me in spite of my illness, I was a stocky boy and a fighter.

My first memory I can recall is when I was about five years old. I was living with my mother in Fredericksburg, Ohio. We lived in a small house with two bedrooms. My mother was a nurse at the local hospital. There was a young woman who would babysit me when my mother was at work. The young woman shared the rent with my mother where we lived. I remember the babysitter making me take naps often. I did not argue with the babysitter, but I would much rather have been outside playing. But the babysitter always told my mother I was a good boy. I have often wondered if my infant and toddler years of being ill was the cause of our family being poor and led to my father and mother separating.

CHAPTER 2

Gaining and Losing an Older Brother

I was wide-eyed with disbelief when my mom said, "Jeffery, we are going to pick up your brother and move to Montezuma, Kansas." It was the last week in June 1958 and I was six years old. We were living in Fredericksburg, Ohio. It was a warm Sunday afternoon, and we just returned home from church when Mom told me the news. I could not believe my ears. With great excitement, I asked Mom, "I have a brother?" Mom replied, "Yes. His name is Alan and he is seven years old."

Mom packed her clothes in one suitcase and my clothes in another suitcase. Mom called a taxi that would take us to the train. The taxi pulled up to our house about twenty minutes later. I was bouncing on the seat of the taxi with excitement to meet my new brother. I asked when we were going to pick up my new brother. Mom told me to relax. Mom told me another family was taking care of Alan. She said they would meet us at the train station.

When we arrived at the train station, Mom went to the counter and purchased our tickets. Mom sat me down on a wooden bench and told me to stay with the luggage. She walked over to some folks and started talking. When she came back to my bench, there was a skinny boy with her carrying a suitcase. Mom told me this was my brother Alan.

I was excited to know I had a new brother. I didn't know how Alan felt about me. But we said "Hi" to each other and hugged. I looked at Alan and I said, "You sure look skinny." Alan replied, "You sure look like a chubby freckled-face Dutch boy." I muttered under my breath, "I'm not a chubby Dutch boy."

We all walked over to the train. The train was huge especially to a boy who was only six years old. The conductor loaded our three suitcases onto the train. We all climbed on board and found our seats. Finally, the train started to move out of the station. I was in awe of the moving train. I kept staring out the window watching the landscape.

After about an hour of riding in the train, Alan was getting bored and started fidgeting. That was when my brother introduced me to a new game. It was called trading punches. Alan said he would punch me in the shoulder. Then I would punch him in the shoulder. Alan said if he punched harder, then I would have to punch him harder. He said this would toughen us up. After trading several punches in the shoulder, I was glad to hear Mom ordering us to stop hitting each other. My shoulder was really starting to hurt.

Alan started fidgeting again and asked Mom if we could go exploring on the train. I guess Mom did not want to see us hitting each other again so she said, "Yes." Alan led the way and off we went from one railcar to another railcar. I was fascinated at the sound the railcars made when we crossed from one railcar to another. There was one railcar that had several tables and people were eating at that railcar. I couldn't wait to tell mom about that railcar. I was getting hungry. Some of the passengers seemed to be getting annoyed at us running up and down the railcars. Alan and I just laughed and kept exploring.

When we got back to our seats, I told Mom about the dinning railcar. I asked if we could go there and get some food. Mom told me to sit down and took some sandwiches out of her bag for us to eat. Then it got dark outside and I couldn't see anything out of the window. I slumped down in my seat and went to sleep.

When I awoke, the train was pulling into a huge train station. Mom told us we had arrived in Chicago, Illinois. Mom told Alan and I that we had to get on a different train for the rest of the trip. We exited the train. I was in awe when I saw several rows of trains. Some of the engines were on and sounded awesome. Some of the engines were off and sitting idle. I was mesmerized as I watched one train start to move and leave the station.

I asked Mom which train we were going to get on. She said our train had not arrived at the train station yet. She said we would have to wait inside the train station until it arrived. Mom said we would have to wait over an hour. Alan said, "We're going exploring." So off we went. The inside of the train station was huge. We had been exploring over an hour. I saw a couple men in sailor uniforms carrying big green bags. They looked at us running around like little heathens. I tried to give the sailors a salute. They both smiled at us and gave me a salute back. I felt like a soldier boy as I was grinning from ear to ear.

Mom finally saw us running down those huge marble stairs they had in the train station. She hollered at us to come over and get on the train. She said it was going to leave in five minutes. We ran over to her all out of breath. Mom looked really angry. We went out to the loading area where all the trains were lined up in a row. Mom told us which train was ours and we climbed aboard and found our seat.

As we were pulling out of the train station, the sun was coming up. Alan and I started discussing which direction we were going. Alan said we were going north. I told him "No, we were going south." Alan said I didn't know what I was talking about. I told Alan the sun comes up in the east. Since the sun was to our left, that meant we were going south. Alan again repeated that I didn't know what I was talking about. I replied, "Alan, you are so dumb."

With that remark, Alan started the "trading punches" game. After trading several punches on the shoulder, Mom hollered, "Stop hitting each other." Again, I was very glad to hear mom ordering us to stop trading punches. My shoulder was very sore and probably turning black and blue. Then Alan said, "Let's go exploring on this train." Off we went exploring. This train looked almost like the other train we were on. It seemed to be a little shorter though. It took us two days to arrive at Dodge City, Kansas. We had to take a bus to our final destination, Montezuma Kansas.

When we arrived at Montezuma Kansas, we stayed with some folks I never saw before. They lived on a farm outside of Montezuma Kansas. We stayed with them for about a week. Then Mom said the folks we were living with would rent us a house with one bedroom in town. Mom told me that we were very poor. Mom told me Alan would be staying with the folks because she could not afford to take care of both of us. I gave my new brother a hug and said goodbye. I felt sad to leave my new brother behind. After all, I had just met him. Reluctantly, I followed my mom to the waiting car.

The folks we had stayed with for almost a week took us into the town of Montezuma, Kansas. They pulled up and stopped in front of a small house. We took our two suitcases and walked into the house. The house had a small living room, small kitchen, small bathroom, and one small bedroom. This was the beginning of our new life. That night, I was thinking about how excited I was to have gained a new older brother and then how sad I was about losing an older brother. Then I thought to myself, "Life isn't very fair. I guess that is just the way life is." And for no reason, I started to cry. Then I said to myself, "Quit being a sissy and toughen up, boy." And went to sleep.

CHAPTER 3

The Stranger

Mom and I had been living in the small house with one bedroom for about two months. It was a hot summer day in the middle of August 1958. Mom told me I would be going to school in the fall. I asked Mom, "What is a school?" Mom said, "It is a place where you will learn things and have other children to play with." She said, "You will be going to the first grade."

I was not impressed. I had no problem playing alone by myself. I had a very good imagination. I was always daydreaming about being a cowboy wearing my colt 45 strapped in my holster. I would straddle a broom pretending I was riding my black stallion. Of course, I had to ride my black stallion outside. The house was too small to ride my horse inside.

Since it was getting hot outside, I went into the small living room to play. I got onto my hands and knees and started playing with my plastic toy car. That is when I heard a knock on the door. Mom was in the kitchen, so I stood up, ran over, and opened the door.

There was a big stocky man with coal black wavy hair standing at the door. The stranger stared at me looking me over from head to toe. I stepped back feeling a little uneasy. The stranger asked if my mom was at home. I said, "Yes, Sir." I shut the door in the man's face and I ran to the kitchen.

I told mom there was a stranger at the door. Mom went to the front door with me following behind her. Mom opened the door that I had closed. I heard her gasp for air and say, "Good Lord." Mom invited the stranger to come in. Mom asked if the stranger would like some coffee. The stranger replied yes and followed her into the kitchen.

I went back to playing with my plastic toy car on the living room floor. Adult conversations were always boring to me. Then I heard Mom crying. My heart started to race. I ran into the kitchen screaming at the stranger to stop hurting my mom. Mom told me to calm down. Mom told me the stranger was not hurting her. Mom wiped the tears away from her eyes. Then Mom said, "This is no stranger. This man is your dad."

I stared at the stranger for a long time. I was in disbelief. Then I asked Mom, "I have a dad?" Mom replied, "Yes, this is your father." The stranger stood up, held out his hands, and said, "Will you come give me a hug, son?" I guess I was so excited to finally have a dad that I went over and gave the stranger a hug. I asked Mom if my new dad would be staying with us. Mom replied "Yes, your dad will be living with us."

My new dad asked how I was doing. I told him I was just fine. I told him I used to have an older brother, but he lives with somebody else now. I told my new dad his name was Alan. My dad said he knew about my older brother and also knew his name was Alan.

He asked me if I would like to have my older brother living back with us. With excitement, I yelled, "Heck yeah."

Two days after my new dad had arrived at my house, we drove to the folks where my brother Alan was staying. My new dad told me to stay in the car. My dad walked briskly up to their house. I could hear the loud knocking on the door from the car. The door opened and dad went inside. He was inside the house for about fifteen minutes.

When he came out of the house, he had my skinny brother Alan with him. Alan was carrying the suitcase that I had seen him with at the train station. Dad drove us back to our house. What a week. I met a stranger and now had a dad and a mom to take care of me. I also had my older brother back to play with. It didn't take long for Alan to re-introduce the game of "punching shoulders." Even though that game got painful from time to time, it was great to have an older brother to play with.

CHAPTER 4

Surprise, Two More Brothers

It was the last weekend in August 1958, when Dad told Mom, Alan and I to sit at the kitchen table. Dad said, "I have something to tell you boys." Dad told us we had two older brothers that were living in Georgia. He said their names were Mike and Bob. He said Mike was the oldest. Mike was ten years old, and Bob was nine years old. I thought, "What a surprise, I have two more brothers. I wondered why Mom never mentioned I had three brothers before." Dad said, "We are leaving early tomorrow morning so you boys can meet your brothers."

That night when we went to bed I asked Alan, "Did you know we had two older brothers?" Alan replied, "First time I heard of it." I asked Alan, "Did you know I was your brother before we met at the train station." Alan said, "The folks I was living with told me I had a younger brother. But I didn't know your name." I said, "You didn't ask the folks you lived with what my name was?" Alan replied, "Nope." I said, "Well, we have two more older brothers, and their names are Mike and Bob." I was so excited I could hardly sleep.

We left before sunrise. Dad drove straight through from Montezuma, Kansas to Georgia. Dad only stopped for gas and food.

It was mid-day Sunday when Dad pulled into a driveway at a huge farmhouse. The farmhouse looked brand new. It was neatly painted along with all the surrounding buildings. I leaned over to Alan and I said, "It looks like these people are rich."

Dad told Alan and I to stay in the car and said, "Do not get out of the car," in a gruff voice. He said he would go get Mike and Bob and we would go somewhere to have a nice picnic. Dad walked up to the farmhouse and knocked on the door. A man opened the door and invited my dad to come inside. Dad was inside the farmhouse about fifteen minutes.

Then dad came out of the farmhouse with two boys following him. Dad got behind the steering wheel. Mike got in the front passenger side of the car. He was the oldest, so he got to ride shotgun. Bob scooted me over and got in the back-seat. Dad introduced the two new older brothers to Alan and me.

I asked dad if we were going to our picnic now. Dad said, "We're going to a picnic all right." We backed out of the farmhouse driveway. Dad accelerated the car and off we headed to our picnic. After driving for about 5 hours, dad pulled into a gas station. He got gas and got some sandwiches. He gave each of us boys a sandwich and said, "This is our picnic. We are going to have our picnic on the road while we're driving." After I ate my food, I started asking Bob a million questions.

I asked Bob, "Did you know you had two younger brothers?" Bob replied, "No, I thought Mike was my only brother." Bob said, "I thought those folks we lived with were our parents." I asked Mike, "Did you know you had two younger brothers?" Mike replied, "I vaguely remember having two younger brothers." Mike added, "But I was very young."

I asked Bob what it was like living in Georgia. Bob said they lived on a big orchard farm. He said it was great. I asked Bob if he lived in that big house they came out of. Bob replied, "Well, of course we did." I told Bob he was going to be in for a big surprise. I told him we lived in a very small home. I told him Alan and I slept in the living room. I said, "It looks like all four of us will be sleeping in the living room."

Then Alan started asking Bob a bunch of questions. I was left out of their conversation. So I leaned against my new older brother, Bob, and went to sleep.

Dad drove straight through from Georgia back to Kansas. Dad only stopped for gas and food. Nowadays, there probably would have been an amber alert put out on my two brothers and our dad.

I remembered thinking back about the stranger knocking on the front door. Then I realized I had met several strangers. I met a stranger at the train station when we left Fredericksburg, Ohio. I met a stranger in Montezuma, Kansas. I met two other strangers in Georgia. All along, the strangers were not strangers at all. The strangers were my new family. Again, I wondered why Mom never mentioned I had a dad and three brothers before I met them. All I knew was we were a family that was reunited.

CHAPTER 5

Moving to the Farm

It was the first week in September 1958. It had been a week since we returned home from Georgia with my brothers Mike and Bob. Having six people living in that small home was very cramped. The four of us boys would sleep in the small living room on the floor. I never understood why Mom kept saying, "I can't wait for school to start." I guess because it was so crowded in that small house. I was not in the least bit interested for school to start.

Although I did not have a problem with playing alone by myself, I was having a great time playing with my brothers. I did start to notice that Mike did not play outside with Bob, Alan, and myself. Mike mostly liked to play board games inside. Mike loved to play board games that included money the best. Mike always won. Mike seemed to be the smartest one of all us boys.

The first weekend after starting school, Dad had another one of his meetings with all of us. Dad said, "Next week, we will be moving out to a farmhouse out on the prairie." He said it needed a lot of repairs. He said we will all have to pitch in to fix it up. Dad said we would have to clear the brush from the house, barn, and storage shed. Dad told us it was a bigger house and we could roam all over the land. We were all excited we were moving out of the small house in Montezuma, Kansas.

The next weekend, we drove out to our new home. The sun was just coming up over the horizon when we drove down a private dirt road that was over half a mile long. We arrived at our new residence. The house was about fifty feet from the dirt driveway.

There was a storage shed located about 100 feet on the left side of the house. On the side of the storage shed were three wired cages containing husked corncobs. Slightly behind and fifty feet to the right of the storage shed was a two-story barn.

On the right side of the barn and about 200 feet behind the house was a wooden arena corral. There were two rows of an electric wire fence spaced about six feet apart running from the barn to the wooden arena corral. Dad told us the arena fence corral was for staging cows for auction to sell them.

Dad was not kidding when he said it needed a lot of repairs. Our new home was a wreck. It looked like it was ready to be demolished. The barn was a wreck also. It needed boards replaced and painted. Inside the barn was filthy. It had junk and trash everywhere. The storage shed was just as bad. The electric wire fence had fallen off some of their posts and were lying on the ground in some areas.

Dad was a no-nonsense type of person. Dad said, "Let's get to work." Dad said, "We would fix the house first, the barn second, and the storage shed third." The dilapidated new home was much bigger than that small house in Montezuma, Kansas. This house had three bedrooms.

Dad said Mike and Bob would have to share one bedroom. Alan and I would have to share the other bedroom by ourselves. Dad told Mike and Bob they would be responsible for fixing up their room. He gave them paint and brushes and told them to get to work. Dad told Alan and I that we would have to paint our room tomorrow. He said he had to repair the holes in the walls with sheetrock in our bedroom first. Dad told us to get a bucket of water and start cleaning the windows.

Dad did not believe in lazy slackers. Dad believed everyone should earn their own keep. Dad would constantly say, "You are a Tracey, earn your own keep." Mom was cleaning the kitchen and Dad was replacing the sheetrock in our room. After Dad replaced the sheetrock, he started clearing the brush and high weeds away from the outside of the house.

When the sun went down, Dad came in the house. Mom had fixed supper. Since there was no furniture in the house, we sat down on the floor to eat. Dad said, "How do you like your new big house?" I was too exhausted to say anything. After I ate, I went to Alan's and my bedroom and went to sleep on the floor.

Like I said, Dad was a no-nonsense type of person. The sun had just come up when Dad came into our room with our paint and brushes. Dad said, "Let's get to work." Alan said, "I'm getting something to eat." Dad said, "After you and Jeffery paint your bedroom." Dad said, "Sooner you get your room painted, the sooner you eat." I was starving, so I got to work painting the walls. I heard Dad tell Mike and Bob to clean the living room before they could eat. While I was painting, I heard Dad up on the roof replacing old and missing shingles. I recalled what Dad always said, "You are a Tracey. You earn your keep."

Alan and I had not completed painting our bedroom when Mom called everyone to the kitchen to eat. Again, we ate our breakfast on the floor. After we ate, Alan and I went back to painting our bedroom. When we completed painting our bedroom, it was afternoon. Dad came in and checked our work. Dad said, "Nice Job."

This is the first time I had a feeling of accomplishing something on my own and someone appreciating it. I was proud of the work I did. I was a Tracey and I earned my keep. It was short lived. Dad said, "Okay, let's start clearing the brushes and weeds away from the barn." When the sun went down, we went in the house and ate supper. I went straight to my bedroom, admired my newly painted bedroom, and fell soundly asleep on the floor.

I was sure glad Monday was a school day. Even though we had to get up at 6:00 a.m., this was going to be a day of rest. We had to walk the half-mile dirt road to where the school bus would pick us up at 7:00 a.m. sharp. Dad would say, "If you miss the bus, you better be ready to walk the ten miles to school." Boy was I wrong about a school day being a day of rest.

As soon as we got home, Dad said, "You boys got a couple of daylight hours to help me clean out the barn." I went to work. I was picking up worn out old tractor parts and placing them on a trailer. I remember Alan and Bob picking up old junk parts and placing them on the trailer. But I don't remember Mike out in the barn helping. I think he was in the house cleaning what needed to be cleaned. It took us the rest of the school week to clean up the trash in the barn. Dad would take the old junk parts to a junkyard and receive money for it.

When the school week finally ended, the barn was finally clean. The last thing we did was to secure the electric wire fence back on their posts. Our work on the barn was finally complete. Dad walked in the barn and looked all around. Dad came out and said, "Boys, job well done." Again, I felt that feeling of accomplishing something on my own and someone appreciating it. Again, I was proud of the work I did. Even though I was six years old, I was a Tracey, and I earned my keep.

I told myself I was going to sleep in on Saturday. However, my dad, being a no-nonsense type of person that he is, awoke Mike and Bob in their bedroom and then came to our bedroom and awoke Alan and I at sunrise. Dad told us boys to clean up the storage shed. The storage shed had brushes and high weeds all around the shed. We all got to work and had all the brushes and high weeds cleared by time for breakfast.

After breakfast, we returned to the storage shed. The storage shed had three sections separated by a three-foot wired caged fence attached to wooded posts at each corner. All the sections contained husked corn cobs. Dad wanted all the husked corn cobs in one section. So Bob climbed in one section of the shed and Alan and I climbed in the other section of the shed. We started picking up the husked corn cobs and throwing them into the third section of the shed.

I think it was Alan who threw the first husked corn cob. I don't mean threw the first husked corn cob into the third section of the shed. But was the first to throw the husked corn cob at me. It hit me on the back of the head and it hurt. So naturally, I threw a husked corn cob at Alan. He ducked and I missed. Alan laughed and threw another husked corn cob hitting me again. Bob got in the action and threw a corn cob at Alan hitting him square in the back. Before you knew it, we had a war going on throwing husked corn cobs at each other. I laughed hysterically whenever my corn cob hit the target whether it was Alan or Bob.

We finally realized we were throwing the husked corn cobs back into the other sections of the shed and on the outside of all the sections. When we realized this was going to cause us more work, we ended the husked corn cob war for now. We all knew we would be having more husked corn cob wars in the future.

By Sunday evening, the storage shed was cleaned up and all the husked corn cobs were in one section. When Dad returned from the junkyard, he came to the storage shed. He looked around and told each of us, "Job well done. Next weekend, we will paint the storage shed and the wooden posts." I was beginning to like that feeling of accomplishment and being proud of the work I did. After all, I was a Tracey and I earned my keep.

A month later, after moving into a farmhouse that looked like it should be demolished, it now looked completely refurbished. I found out later in life that my dad had made an agreement with the owner of the farmhouse. The owner had agreed to let us rent the farmhouse free for six months if we fixed up the farm. The owner paid for the supplies needed for the repair. After all, we were a Tracey, and we earned our keep.

CHAPTER 6

The Merry-Go-Round

It was September 1959. It was the first week of school. I was seven years old, and I was just starting the third grade. I already didn't care for school. Therefore, I was not in a good mood. I was glad when the first recess bell rang. I was ready for a break.

I ran outside and jumped on the monkey-bars. I was resting on top of the monkey-bars when I spotted the merry-go-round. The merry-go-round was empty. I climbed off the monkey-bars. I was walking to the merry-go-round when a big girl jumped on and sat on the edge of the merry-go-round. Another big girl started pushing her around in circles by grabbing the rails and shoving them forward. This looked like fun. I was pretending the merry-go-round was a runaway stagecoach. I was going to go galloping up to the stagecoach on my black stallion horse. I would jump off my horse and onto the stagecoach. I was going to save the girl on the runaway stagecoach.

I started to run on the side of the revolving merry-go-round. Just as I was getting ready to jump on the merry-go-round, the big girl sitting on the merry-go-round came around where I was. The big girl stuck out both her legs straight out and kicked me in the chest. She knocked the wind out of me and I fell to the ground. I gasped for air. I got angry. I jumped up and I started running around the merry-go-round. When the big girl was on the opposite side of the merry-go-round, I jumped on. I landed hard and grabbed a rail to hang on. The other big girl was still pushing on the rails to keep the merry-go-round revolving.

I crawled up to the center of the merry-go-round. The big girl that knocked the wind out of me was sitting with her back to me. I got in a sitting position and I slid down directly behind the big girl. I quickly coiled my legs and placed my feet on her back. I pushed my legs straight out hard and shoved that big girl right off the merry-go-round. I thought, "That will teach her to kick me to the ground."

The big girl got up crying and ran to the teacher. She told the teacher I hit her off the merry-go-round. The teacher looked the big girl over. The teacher patted her on the head and told her she would be okay. The big girl went over to her friend and they went off skipping and laughing.

The teacher walked briskly over to me. I was still sitting on the merry-go-round. Since no one was pushing the merry-go-round, it had come to a slow stop. I had saved the stagecoach. I was snapped out of my daydream. The teacher bent over me and took her thumb and forefinger and clamped it hard against my earlobe. She jerked me off the merry-go-round by my earlobe. I screamed out, "Ow, ouch, ouchee." I thought my ear was going to tear off.

The teacher yelled at me, "Didn't anyone ever tell you not to hit a girl?" I replied, "No, ma'am." The teacher said, "Well, I've never. What kind of parents do you have?" I replied, "A mom and dad." That response got another jerk on my earlobe. The teacher said, "Recess is over for you, young man." She was walking me back to the classroom. She was walking me back to the classroom very fast. I was having a very hard time keeping up with her. With her hand clamped on my earlobe, I had no choice but to keep up. My head was tilted upward and slightly sideways with my earlobe clenched tightly in her hand. My hand involuntarily reached up and tried to pull her arm down to lessen the pain on my earlobe. I was unsuccessful. Every few steps, the teacher gave my earlobe a little jerk upward. I think she did this just to hear me scream, "Ouch, ouchee, ow."

We finally got to the classroom. The teacher did not sit me down in the first seat in the first row. Oh no, I think she was enjoying pulling my earlobe. The teacher marched me down to the last row of seats by the window. The teacher's thumb and forefinger were still clamped hard on my earlobe. She marched me down to the last seat in the last row with her hand clamped hard on my earlobe. Finally, she let go of my red aching earlobe. The teacher said, "Sit down and do not get up. Your recess is over."

The teacher looked down at me and asked, "Why did you hit that girl off the merry-go-round?" I said, "I didn't hit her off the merry-go-round. I shoved her off the merry-go-round for kicking me in the chest. She knocked the wind out of me when I tried to get on the merry-go-round." The teacher said, "That is no excuse for hitting a girl. Do you understand?" I looked at my teacher giving her my sad brown eyes look and replied, "Yes, ma'am."

Except for the pulling on my earlobe, this punishment wasn't so bad. I was sitting in my desk daydreaming about being Wyatt Earp's deputy. I was riding my black stallion horse. I had just saved a stagecoach. Now I was chasing a bunch of gunslingers for robbing a bank. My daydream was abruptly interrupted when the students walked into the classroom. I guess recess was finally over.

The students started taking their seats. I saw that big girl walking to the last row of seats. Then the big girl started walking down the last row of seats toward me. She was smirking at me and murmured, "Hah, hah, you got in trouble." I could tell she got great pleasure watching the teacher escort me back to the classroom by my earlobe. To my disgust, she kept walking toward me. The big girl plopped down in the seat directly in front of me.

The big girl sitting directly in front of me had two ponytails hanging from the back of her head. I stared at the big girl's ponytail dangling from the back of her head. I could not resist it anymore. My right hand grabbed her right ponytail and I quickly jerked it down hard. She screamed out and started to cry. I think she was fake crying.

The teacher jerked her head around to where the screaming was coming from. The teacher saw the big girl crying. Then the teacher saw me. The teacher's face turned from a soothing face to a scowling face. The teacher picked up a twelve-inch ruler from her desk. She marched straight toward me with the ruler swinging back and forth as she walked. The teacher towered over me glaring. She ordered, "Put your hands flat on top of the desk." I knew I was in trouble again. I looked at her with my big sad brown eyes and said, "Yes, ma'am." Sometimes that worked. But not this time. The teacher took that ruler and whacked my hands three hard times. The teacher said, "Didn't I tell you a man never hits a girl?" I replied, "I didn't hit her. I pulled her ponytail." That reply got me another two smacks on the back of my hands.

Since I was a young boy and only had brothers, I didn't quite understand why you couldn't at least pull their ponytail until after I grew up. I was beginning to think that life was not really fair. That teacher taught me a valuable lesson I won't ever forget. Even if a girl hits me, a man never hits a girl.

CHAPTER 7

The Tractor

It was October 1959. Our task was to clean the fields from debris so the neighbor could cultivate the fields for planting crops next spring. Dad borrowed a tractor and flatbed trailer from the neighbor. Dad drove the tractor and Bob, Alan, and I picked up the debris in the fields. When we came to some heavy rocks, Dad would have to stop the tractor, get off, and help dig out the heavy rocks. Then we would load the rocks onto the flatbed. Finally, Dad showed us how to drive the tractor. Bob drove the tractor first. About an hour later, Alan drove the tractor. We picked up a pile of rocks and boards and loaded them on the flatbed trailer. We came across an empty fifty- gallon metal drum. We all wondered who dumped that metal drum out in the field. Dad mumbled under his breath, "I wonder what was in that drum." We lifted the metal drum onto the flatbed trailer and kept on working.

At noon, Mom came walking out to the field with some sand-wiches. After eating, Dad said, "Okay, Jeffery it's your turn to drive the tractor. We're going to drive mom back to the house." I replied, "I don't know how to drive the tractor." Dad said, "It's time you learn." Dad climbed on the tractor and showed me the gear shift. He showed me how the slots in the gear shift looked like a capital (H). Dad showed me how to shift the gears into reverse, first gear, second gear, and third gear. Dad showed me how to push in the clutch all the way to the floor when I moved the gear shift. Dad then said okay, "It's all yours to drive."

Mom was standing on the flatbed trailer when I started to drive. Dad was sitting on the side of the tractor fender. Dad said, "Push in the clutch and slide the gear shift to first." I did what he asked me to do. He then told me to push on the gas pedal and let the clutch out slowly. I pressed down on the gas pedal and was slowly lifting the clutch when it slipped off my foot. The tractor jerked violently forward.

Mom screamed as she fell off the flatbed trailer. I turned around to see the fifty-gallon drum narrowly miss her head by inches. Dad jumped off the tractor and ran to Mom. Dad helped Mom get up and saw she was not seriously hurt.

Dad screamed at me to stop the tractor. Then I panicked. I didn't know how to stop the tractor. I cried back to Dad, "How do I stop the tractor?" Dad yelled, "Step on the brake." I didn't know where the brake pedal was. I kept stepping down on the clutch but the tractor kept on moving. Finally, Dad came running up to the moving tractor and jumped on and stopped the tractor.

I was crying and asked, "Is Mom okay?" Dad said, "She will be sore and have some bruises but she will be okay." I was done driving the tractor for that day. Dad turned the tractor around to where Mom, Bob, and Alan were standing. I ran over to Mom and gave her a hug and said I was sorry. I never understood why she asked me a weird question. She asked, "Are you and Dad trying to kill me?" I started to sob and said, "No way, Mom. I didn't know how to drive the tractor." Mom said, "I was just wondering why your dad would let you drive when I was on the trailer? Especially since you did not know how." I didn't know what to say to that. So I just gave Mom a great big hug and said I was sorry.

CHAPTER 8

Flip-Flop, Flip-Flop

It was April 1960, and I just turned eight years old. I could hardly wait for school to be out for the summer. Our elementary school was putting on class plays. I do not remember what the third grade theme play was about. But it involved a train moving across the huge stage. I was a very quiet and shy person at eight years old. I did not like to give speeches or perform any kind of acting roles on the stage. I especially did not like to perform in front of a large audience.

I told my third grade teacher I did not want to be in the play. I told my teacher that my family was poor. I did not have any new clothes to wear and my shoes were falling apart. My teacher hugged me and patted me on the back. She told me not to worry.

She told me the play was about a train going up a hill. She said there would be three other third graders in the play. The first student would be the locomotive, the second student would be a tanker railcar, and the third student would be a cargo railcar. She said I was going to be the caboose at the end of the train. She said I would be carrying a big cardboard box that looked like the caboose railcar.

My teacher told me I did not need new clothes. The audience would not see my clothes because I would be in a huge cardboard box that looked like a caboose. My teacher told me there would be a red line in the middle of the stage. When I crossed the red line, I had to say, "I am the caboose and I am the last railcar on a train."

I was walking home from school the day before the play. The sole on my left shoe came loose. It made a flip-flop sound every time I took a step. I practiced walking on the tip of my toes to keep my shoes from making the flip-flop sound. It still made the flip-flop sound when I lifted up my foot to take the next step. When I got home, I found a brown one-fourth-inch wide rubber band. I wrapped the rubber band around the sole and shoe a couple of times. This secured the sole to my shoe. I walked around the house. I did not hear any flip-flopping sound when I took my steps.

I took my dad's black shoe polish and I polished the brown rubber band to match the color of my black shoe. I must admit it looked pretty good. You could barely see the rubber band wrapped around my shoe. I was pretty proud of my accomplishment. I went to school the next day with the rubber band wrapped around my shoe. My shoe was quiet. There were no flip-flopping sounds. I was ready to perform in the play.

Our third grade teacher had the four of us get together on the right side of the stage behind the curtain. She had us say our lines one last time. I got into my large cardboard box caboose railcar. I kept repeating my lines, "I am the caboose and the last railcar on a train," over and over again so I would not forget. Then the curtain opened. We started walking across the huge stage in front of the audience. I had about fifteen feet to go before I reached the red line where I had to say my line. That was when my rubber band busted. I heard the horrible flip-flop sound against the stage's hardwood floor. I could hear flip-flop, flip-flop, flip-flop with each step I took. The sound seemed to be getting louder with each step I took. I was fighting back my tears when I reached the red line for my speech. My voice was quivering when I choked out the words, "I'm, I'm a caboose." I was so embarrassed because of my flip-flopping shoe I forgot the rest of my line. I pushed the cardboard railcar in front of me so I could get off the huge stage. I dreaded the forty feet I would have to cross to exit the stage. Each step I took, I heard the horrible flip-flop, flip-flop, flip-flop sound my shoe made. I had about ten more feet to walk when I heard chuckling coming from the audience. I heard a woman say, "His parents should have bought him some new shoes." I knew they were laughing at me. I fiercely fought back my tears but was unsuccessful. By the time I exited the stage, I had tears streaming down my cheeks.

It never occurred to me that the rubber band might bust. I told myself I would never speak to my third grade teacher again for making me perform in that play. I tore off that stupid cardboard caboose box. I ran home with my left shoe flip-flopping all the way. I hated that we had to be so poor. I vowed to never laugh at or make fun of people that are poor.

CHAPTER 9

The Rocking Car

It was the first week in June 1961. I was nine years old. We had just heard our dad say he was going to Cimarron, Kansas. Dad asked if we would like to go. He said we could go swimming in their public swimming pool. It had a high and low diving board. We all jumped up and down like wild animals and screamed, "YES." We all climbed into the beat up old 1952 Chevy. Since Mike was the oldest, he got to ride shotgun. Bob, Alan, and I climbed into the back-seat. Since I was the youngest, I had to sit in the middle of the back-seat.

Dad started the beat up old Chevy and off we headed to Cimarron, Kansas forty miles away. The first ten miles were full of excitement and anticipation of diving off the high and low diving board. The next five miles was pure boredom. If you ever traveled on a highway in Kansas, you know what I mean. Kansas is a flat prairie land. The highways are straight and long. Alan started it all. Alan bumped into my shoulder, I bumped into Bob's shoulder and Bob bumped into the side of the car. Then Bob bumped into my shoulder, I bumped back into Alan's shoulder and Alan bumped into the other side of the car. Alan repeated bumping into me, I repeated bumping into Bob and Bob repeated bumping into the side of the car. After about the fourth session of bumping back and forth, we felt the car start rocking back and forth. That did it. All three of us went into high gear bumping back and forth. This really started the car rocking back and forth while dad was driving down the highway.

Dad told us to stop rocking the car, but we just laughed. Dad then tried to swat at us. We just leaned back in the seat still rocking the car and laughing hysterically. Suddenly, the car pulled over to the side of the road and stopped. I thought, "Uh, oh, we're in trouble now." Dad had enough of us rocking the car. Dad made us lean over the backseat and gave us a smack on the butt. The first mile back on the highway, we were sitting very still and quiet. The second mile, I was still thinking of the smack on my butt. The third mile was getting boring. We almost made it to the fourth mile when Alan started the bumping process again. We all giggled and had the car rocking in no time. Dad yelled at us to stop rocking the damn car. We just laughed harder and kept rocking the car.

Dad pulled the car off the highway again and stopped. I thought we were in for a good spanking this time. But Dad just stayed in the driver's seat and said, "You boys want to rock the car? Then start rocking the car." Well, let me tell you, trying to rock a car weighing 3,300 pounds sitting still is not easy. We kept bumping into each other shoulders but the car would barely rock. What seemed like an hour and after both my shoulders were hurting, Dad asked if we were done rocking the car. We all replied, "Yes, sir." Dad asked one more time. "Are you sure you're done rocking the car." We all replied, "Yes, sir." Dad put the car in gear and pulled back on the highway.

For the next five miles, we were sitting still and were quiet as a mouse. After five or six more miles, the car hit a bump in the road and started swaying. We started giggling and could not help ourselves. Before we knew it, the car was rocking again. Dad would have no part of it. He yelled back and said, "That's it. I am turning this damn rocking car around and we are going home." Mike turned around and said, "You boys ruin everything. You are so immature."

That got our attention. We each told dad how very sorry we were. We each promised Dad that we would not rock the car ever again. Dad was able to drive the remaining ten miles to Cimarron Kansas in peace and quiet. I was very thankful dad put up with three very ornery boys. Dad dropped us off at the public swimming pool. We had a blast diving off the low and high diving board. But I will never forget the fun I had in the rocking car. We kept our promise. We never rocked the car again.

CHAPTER 10

The Howling Camping Trip

It was the last week in August 1961. I was almost a grownup or so I thought. I was nine years old. My two older brothers; Bob was twelve, Alan was ten, and myself decided to have one more camping trip before school started. I took off the two sheets from our bed and tightly rolled them up. Since we were poor, we had to make do with what we had. Those two sheets were our tent. I always imagined I was carrying a real army tent and not a couple of sheets. I strapped my hunting knife to my waist with my belt. I gave Bob and Alan their hunting knives.

We made popcorn to eat at our campfire. We had a big brown paper grocery bag full of popcorn. We poured melted butter and sprinkled salt all over the popcorn. Then we shook the bag full of popcorn. You could see buttery spots outside the popcorn brown paper bag. The popcorn smelled delicious. In fact, it smelled so delicious, I could not help myself. I grabbed a big handful of that delicious smelling popcorn and shoved it into my mouth. Unfortunately, my brothers saw me. Both Bob and Alan punched me in the shoulder reprimanding me. Bob said, "Jeff, the popcorn is for the campfire."

Since I was the youngest, I had the privilege of carrying the gear. I had the rolled up sheets under my left arm. I was holding the delicious smelling popcorn in my right hand. We headed out in the

Kansas flat prairie landscape. We hiked about forty-five minutes. We passed the gullies where we played and found Indian arrowheads. We hiked among the cactuses watching out for snakes. We came to a flat grassy area. There were some dead dried cactus limbs and scattered tree limbs on the ground. Bob said, "We will set up camp here."

We all gathered up the tree limbs to prop up our bedsheets to make our tent and for our campfire. It was getting dark by the time we had the sheets secured tightly on the limbs. Then we got the campfire going. We sat around the campfire. We were all munching on that delicious smelling popcorn. Bob and Alan took turns telling stories late into the night. Some of the stories were funny. Some of the stories were scary. But we were having a blast.

It was during one of the scary stories, when I got scared. I thought I heard an animal behind our tent. I asked Bob if he heard the noise. Bob and Alan went to the back of the tent and looked into the dark. All they heard was some howling far away. Bob said, "Sounds like some dogs but they were far away." We went back to munching on the delicious popcorn. Bob and Alan continued telling stories way past midnight.

Then Bob noticed the sound of howling dogs behind our tent were getting closer. Then the howling dogs seemed to spread outwards toward the side of our campsite. Bob said we needed to make some weapons to be on the safe side. There were cactus bushes nearby our campsite. The cactuses were about four inches in diameter, round and flat with thorns protruding out. Bob told us to cut off the cactuses from the bushes with our hunting knives. Bob then told us to cut a slit in the middle of the cactus. Bob told us to take the belt and slip it through the cactus and looped it through the belt buckle. Now we had a weapon.

Then the howling dogs seemed to be encircling the campsite. Bob said, "We have to leave now before the dogs circle us completely." We all started running toward home. We left the delicious popcorn and the tent by the campsite. We were yelling and hollering to scare the howling dogs away. The whole time we were swinging our belt buckle holding those cactuses wildly. We were hoping to hit one of those howling dogs if they got to close. But we only succeeded in hitting our own legs and thighs with the thorns.

We finally arrived at the house exhausted and out of breath. Then we noticed the pain. We had lodged several thorns in our legs, thighs and butts. It was from swinging those cactuses around and around while running wildly. Bob got the pliers and started pulling out the thorns on me and Alan. Alan then took the pliers and pulled the thorns embedded in Bob's leg and thigh.

The next day, we went back to our campsite to get our tent (bed sheets). We took our weapons (cactuses) still attached to our belts. When we arrived at the campsite, the bed sheets were torn and laying in a heap on the ground. The popcorn bag was shredded. All the popcorn was gone. Bob said it must have been the smell of our popcorn that brought the wild dogs. We picked up the bed sheets and took them back home. We knew we were lucky and made the right decision to leave the campsite when we did.

The next day, some neighbors told Dad there was a pack of hyenas roaming the area. We knew then that the howling we heard was from that pack of hyenas. I guess hyenas liked our popcorn as much as we did. I will never forget that howling camping trip.

CHAPTER 11

The Electric Fence

It was the first warm weekend in May 1962. I was now ten years old. There had just been a spring shower that moved through the area. Whenever it rained, the gulleys about a mile from our farmhouse would flood. Bob said another big thunderstorm was coming our way. Bob said, "The next big thunderstorm should fill up the gullies." My brothers Bob and Alan suggested we should make a raft and float down the gulley's river. This sounded like a great idea to me. "What an adventure," I thought. I hollered, "Let's go."

We went to the barn and found some loose boards. Bob found some old ropes. Bob was the leader of our group. Alan was second in command. Although sometimes Alan acted like he was the leader. I was last in command. So naturally, I got the pleasure of carrying the loose boards and ropes out to the gulley.

When we headed out toward the prairie where the gullies were located, we would have to crawl under two rows of electrified fence wires. The electric wire went from the barn to the cattle staging arena. The two rows of electric wires were six feet apart creating a pathway for the cows to follow. The electric wires had low voltage of electricity flowing through them. The electric wire would not harm you, but it would give you quite a jolt. It would deter the cows from wandering away from the pathway. The cows would be prodded to move from the barn to the cattle arena. They would be staged there for auction and sold.

Sometimes, when we got bored and had nothing to do, we would play the electric game. Bob, Alan, and myself would try to see who could hold onto the electric wire the longest. I never cared that much about pain, so I was always the first to let go of the electric wire. Alan would always laugh and call me a sissy, I would always mutter back, "I'm not a sissy. I'm just smarter." But as I look back, I am not so sure I was smarter. I always grabbed the electric fence wire with Alan and Bob when we played the electric game.

I followed Bob and Alan carrying the loose boards and rope to the electric fence wires. Bob crawled under the first electric wire. He stood up and walked the six feet over to the second electric wire before dropping on his hands and knees and crawling under. Bob then stood up and waited for the rope and boards. Alan crawled under the first electric wire and stood up. Alan told me to hand the loose boards and ropes over the electric fence wire. I handed Alan the ropes over the top of the first electric wire. Alan then walked over to the second electric wire. Alan handed the ropes over the top of the second electric wire to Bob.

Alan came back to the first electric wire. As I was handing over the loose boards over the electric wire, my arm touched the electric wire. As I was getting shocked, I yelled out and dropped the loose boards. Some of the loose boards fell on Alan's side of the electric fence wire and some of the loose boards fell on my side. Alan laughed at me getting shocked and picked up the loose boards on his side and walked them over to the second electric wire. He handed the loose boards he had over the second electric wire to Bob.

Alan came back to the first electric wire for the remaining loose boards. I made sure I lifted the remaining loose boards high enough over the electric wire not to get shocked. As Alan took the remaining loose boards, I was never sure but it felt like Alan tried to push the boards down so I would touch the electric wire again. But I jerked my arms back. Alan took the remaining boards over to Bob and handed them over the second electric wire.

I got down on my hands and knees and crawled under the first electric wire. I stood up and walked the six feet over to the second electric wire. I got down on my hands and knees and crawled under the second electric wire. When I got up, the loose boards and rope were lying in a pile.

Like I said, since I was last in command, I got the pleasure of carrying the loose boards and ropes. After carrying the loose boards and rope for about a half mile, I asked Alan. "Will you carry the loose boards and rope the rest of the way." Alan replied, "Quit complaining and toughen up sissy." I muttered, "I'm not a sissy," and carried the loose boards and rope the rest of the way to the gulley.

When we arrived at the gulley, the gulley only had a little rain water flowing downstream. Bob said, "The big thunderstorm is almost here and should fill up the gulley with rain water." We looked to the north and saw that the whole sky was black with huge dark clouds.

Bob wound the rope in and around each board on one end of the raft. Alan wound the rope in and around each board on the other end of the raft. Alan ran out of rope for the last couple of boards. Bob told us to take off our belts and strap the remaining boards together. After about five minutes, we had the raft ready to go.

We took off our shoes, shirt, and pants leaving us in our underwear. We lowered the raft down in the muddy gulley. Bob and Alan held onto the raft on either side to keep it from floating down the gulley. We were waiting excitedly for the big thunderstorm to flood the gulley. We were ready to have the ride of our life on our homemade raft.

I was the first to hear someone yelling at us. I turned around and saw Dad storming toward us screaming his head off. Dad yelled, "Don't you see this huge thunderstorm coming? Why aren't you boys running to the house?" I saw how angry Dad was. I wasn't about to back talk. But I did think, "Duh, yeah we see the big thunderstorm coming. How do you think we are going to go rafting down the gulley?"

Dad screamed at Bob and Alan. "Get out of the gulley immediately and run as fast as you can back to the house right now." Dad turned around and saw me looking bewildered. Dad yelled at me, "Why are you still standing there? Get your butt to the house now." I turned around and started running as fast as I could. It wasn't long when Bob ran past me just in his underwear. Then Alan ran past me just in his underwear. I thought they looked funny running just in their underwear even though I was also running just in my underwear.

I guess I slowed the pace when I started chuckling. Dad was following right behind me. I don't know if he heard me chuckling or if he noticed I slowed my pace down. Whatever it was, I received a smack on the butt with his belt. I immediately picked up my pace. As we were running back to the house, it started raining. The rain was stinging my face and body as I tried to keep up with Bob and Alan. My dad assisted me in not letting me fall too far behind Bob and Alan. Every once in a while, I would receive a smack on the butt with his belt. That motivated me not to fall too far behind Alan and Bob.

When we got close to the barn, it began raining harder. We were all soaking wet. Then I saw Bob yell out and jerk backward. I knew Bob must have run into the first electric fence wire. I saw Bob get down on his hands and knees and crawl under both rows of the electric wires. Bob then stood up and ran to the house.

Then I saw Alan yell out and jerk backward. I knew Alan must have run into the first electric wire. I saw Alan get down on his hands and knees and crawl under both rows of the electric wires. Then Alan stood up and ran to the house.

I made up my mind. I was not going to be an idiot like my brothers. I was not going to run into those electric fence wires. I would drop to my hands and knees before I hit the electric fence wire. I would crawl under both rows of the electric wires. I would not be an idiot like my brothers.

Just as I made that final thought, BAMM, I felt like I was getting electrocuted. I screamed out and jerked back just like my idiot brothers did. The electric shock was intensified since we were soaking wet from the rain. Just like my idiot brothers did, I dropped to my hands and knees and crawled under the electric fence wire. I crawled for what seemed forever. When I knew I was well past the second electric fence wire, I jumped up and started running to the house. I took one step and BAMM, I got electrocuted again. I had hit the second electric fence wire. I screamed out and jerked back. I got on my hands and knees crawled under the second electric fence wire.

As I stood up, I was never sure, but I thought I heard my dad chuckling. I don't know what he would be chuckling at. I didn't see anything funny about getting electrocuted. As I was running to the house, I thought, "I'm the idiot. I was the only one who ran into both rows of the electric fence wires." I knew one thing for sure. I would never play the electric game again.

CHAPTER 12

The Dirty School Bus

Spring thunderstorms were popping up daily. It was one of the wettest and muddiest weeks in Montezuma, Kansas history. I remembered seeing my brother Alan's essay describing the condition. His essay was titled "It was Mud." Alan's teacher had taken his class to the state fair that week. He instructed the class to complete a five-hundred-word essay about their experience at the state fair. The teacher posted Alan's essay on the blackboard. The teacher wrote, "How NOT to write a 500 words essay" and placed a LARGE RED "F" on the top of his essay. Alan's teacher was not amused with his title "IT WAS MUD" and even less amused with the essay itself. The essay stated, "It was mud, mud, mud, mud" . . . repeated five-hundred times and then signed, "The end."

Alan's teacher made a point to let me know he did not expect that kind of essay from me. I couldn't help but to chuckle every time I saw Alan's essay with that big fat red "F" posted on the front of the blackboard for everyone to see. And each time I thought, "Alan, you are so dumb."

Like I said, spring thunderstorms were popping up daily that week. It was Friday, and we were excited for being out of school for the weekend. The rain had just ended and the sun was out and shinning. However, all the dirt roads were still very muddy.

Since we lived out on the farm, we rode the school bus home. We had one of the coolest school bus drivers ever. One time, he picked my brother up when his bike tire went flat on the way to school. He put the bike in the aisle in back of the school bus. Like I said, he was really a cool bus driver.

Mike and Bob had taken their bikes to school on this Friday. Alan and myself were riding the school bus home. We were the last students to be dropped off. We were about two miles from home when the school bus started sliding in the mud. The bus driver did everything he could to keep from sliding into the ditch but was unsuccessful. The bus driver immediately turned around in his seat and asked if we were okay. He knew we were okay when he saw Alan and I were laughing hysterically. We thought it was cool being stuck in the ditch.

Alan and I stood up from our seats and walked to the front of the bus. The bus driver stepped out of the school bus to assess the situation. As Alan and I were stepping out of the school bus, the bus driver turned around and ordered us back into the school bus. He told Alan and me he would have to go to the nearest farm and get help. He told Alan and me to stay in the bus and not leave. I told him, "Yes, sir." I went and sat in the front seat. Alan told the bus driver we could walk home. The bus driver told Alan not to walk home. He said he was responsible for our safety until he dropped us off at our destination. Alan climbed back into the bus disappointed.

After about fifteen minutes, Alan got bored and stepped out of the bus. I told Alan we were instructed to stay in the school bus. Alan said, "So what." Alan started walking around the bus. I stepped out of the bus to see what Alan was doing. When I walked around the left front fender of the school bus, I got hit in the shoulder with a mud ball. Alan laughed with pride after hitting his mark. I scooped up some mud and threw it at Alan. He ducked and I missed. I quickly scooped up some more mud and hurled it at Alan and hit him on the leg.

That started the mud war. Alan would throw a barrage of mud balls at me. Some of the mud balls would strike me; others would miss and land on the side of the bus. I would retaliate and throw a barrage of mud balls at Alan. Most of the mud balls would miss Alan and land on the side of the school bus including on the windows. Alan was skinny and quick. But every once in a while, I would hit my target. I was stocky and slower. Alan hit his target more often than he missed.

After being covered in mud and tired of being hit with mud balls, I took refuge in the school bus. I sat down in the second row seat behind the steering wheel. Alan would have no part of it. I guess he took offense to me hitting him with a few mud balls. He was not about to end this mud war. He stepped in the school bus and threw a barrage of mud balls at me. One mud ball hit me on top of the head as I was ducking behind the seat.

Alan went outside to get more mud balls. I took this opportunity to run out the rear exit door. I scooped up a lot of mud and made several mud balls and laid them on the floor by the rear exit door. As Alan came down the school bus aisle, I threw a barrage of mud balls. I landed a few mud balls on my target. Most of the mud balls landed on the interior seats and interior windows on the school bus.

Alan would fire a barrage of mud balls at me. I used the rear exit door as my shield. I would open the door to fire my mud balls at Alan. Then close the door when he fired his mud balls. Every once in a while, Alan would hit his target. But the rear exit door caught the majority of the mud balls.

The mud ball fight war was going on so strong, we did not hear the tractor driving up behind us. I had just fired a mud ball and hit my target when I heard someone behind me yell. "What the hell is wrong with you, boys?"

I stopped firing my mud balls at Alan and turned around. I thought, "Uh-oh. We're in big trouble now," when I saw the school bus driver standing behind me. Just about then, a mud ball came flying out the rear exit door. It almost hit the school bus driver. The school bus driver walked around the school bus. Then he stepped inside the school bus and looked in horror. When he stepped out of the dirty school bus, he shook his head and stood in shock and disbelief. He could not believe his school bus could be covered with this much mud inside and out. Our cool school bus driver looked at us and yelled, "You boys will never ride my bus again."

After the school bus driver had his initial shock and awe of how two boys could make this big of a mess on his school bus, he walked over to the man on the tractor. The man on the tractor shook his head and looked disgusted at us. Our cool bus driver instructed us to stand on the other side of the road. They pulled the tractor in front of the school bus and hooked up a chain to the front bumper. Within five minutes, they had the dirty school bus back on the muddy road. They unhooked the chain and the man on the tractor drove away.

Our "pissed off" cool bus driver came over to where we were standing. He glared at us. He said, "Get in the school bus right now and sit down." We both said, "Yes, sir." We climbed in the bus and sat down in the first row of seats. We sat perfectly still and didn't speak a word. Our "pissed off" cool bus driver drove the remaining two miles to our destination.

He stopped the bus. Alan and I stood up to exit the dirty school bus. Our "pissed off" cool bus driver did not open the door. He looked at both of us. He said, "Both of you will be at the school yard at 7:00 a.m. tomorrow and wash this dirty school bus inside and out." He asked, "Do both of you understand?" Alan replied, "Tomorrow is not a school day, it's Saturday." Our "pissed off" cool school bus driver replied, "So what? You will both be there and clean this dirty school bus. I will tell your parents you have detention all day so you will have plenty of time to clean this dirty school bus. You will do this if you boys ever want to ride the school bus again."

I think our cool school bus driver lessened the severity of our dirty school bus stunt to our parents. Because if Dad had known what Alan and I did that day, I am sure both our butts would have met the belt several times.

The next day, Dad dropped us off at the front of the school. Dad said, "This better be your last detention day you ever receive," and drove off.

As we were walking up to the school, our cool school bus driver met us. Our cool bus driver had parked the dirty school bus behind our school. He walked us around to the back of the school. Alan and

I saw the dirty school bus. We looked at each other in disbelief. There was no way we could have made that kind of mess. That dirty school bus was covered in mud from the front bumper to the back bumper.

Our cool bus driver gave us a couple of pails of water and sponges and said, "Wait till you see the inside of the dirty school bus." It took Alan and I all day to clean that dirty school bus. Our cool school bus driver walked up after we had finished cleaning the dirty school bus. He walked completely around the outside of the school bus. Then he stepped inside the school bus. It took him several minutes to inspect the inside of the school bus. He exited the school bus. He looked at both of us. He said, "Job well done. I guess both of you can ride my school bus again." I was relieved to hear we could ride the bus to school.

I was exhausted when we finished. I knew one thing for sure. I would never have another mud fight on a school bus. I will never forget the image I had when I first saw that dirty school bus on that Saturday detention day. To say it was a dirty school bus is putting it mildly. I was thankful that our cool school bus driver allowed us to continue riding his school bus after our famous mud war.

CHAPTER 13

Skinned Alive

I would be really surprised if we went a day my brothers and I did not play "Tag You're It." My brother Bob and Alan got creative in playing "Tag You're It." When we played "Tag You're It," you had rules to follow. We always had to draw sticks to see who was "it" first. Whoever drew the shortest stick was "it" to start the game.

For instance, when we played "Tag You're It" on the fence you had to run on top of the fence. If you fell off the fence, then you were automatically "it." The fence we played on was a cattle staging arena. The arena was a circular wooden fence about 70 feet in diameter. The arena had 4" x 4" posts every 4 feet. The top rung on the fence was a 6' by 4" by ½" cedar picket board nailed sideways to the 4" x 4" posts. There were three rows of the cedar picket boards about two feet apart. At one end of the arena, there was a gate that would swing out away from the arena. The length of the gate was five feet. When the gate was shut and latched, it would be secured but could sway a little if you leaned against it. The cedar picket boards were secured tightly against the 4 x 4 posts.

Bob, Alan, and I played on that fence day after day. Mike was always studying his books. I guess that is why he was the smart one. We would walk on top of the half-inch wide cedar picket fence from post to post. We could walk across the top of the gate. Our balance got so good we could run from post to post on top of the cedar picket fence. So naturally we played "Tag You're It." Like I said, the rules on this game were simple. If you touched another person, they were tagged and were "it." If you fell off the fence, you were automatically "it."

It was hot July day when we were up there on the arena fence playing "Tag You're It." I guess I didn't eat a heavy breakfast that morning. I was running pretty fast on top of the picket fence. I was keeping my balance and not falling off the fence. Alan had just fallen off the fence and was automatically "it." Alan climbed back up to the top of the picket fence and started chasing me.

Like I said, I was running pretty fast and keeping my balance. I got to the gate. Whenever you crossed the gate, you had to take your time because the gate was not as secure as the rest of the fence. As I got in the middle of the gate, the gate started to sway. I glanced back and saw Alan take his foot and was trying to shake the gate so I would fall off and automatically be "it." If I had not glanced back, I might not have missed stepping on the gate fence and losing my balance. But I did. My right foot missed the top of the gate as it swayed.

The right side of my body slid right down the side of the top picket fence. The picket fence peeled off the top layer of my skin from above my hip to the bottom of my underarm. I hit the ground in agony. I got up screaming and running around in circles trying to tear off my shirt. Bob sensed something was wrong and jumped off the fence and ran over to me. Bob saw the blood oozing onto my shirt. Bob helped me take off the shirt. I heard Bob say, "You'll be okay." But I saw the look on Bob's and Alan's faces. They didn't look so convincing.

Bob and Alan helped me walk to the house. Bob told me to lie down on my bed. Bob told me my wound was not that deep. He said my bleeding had stopped. Bob reassured me that I would be okay. Bob got a washrag and washed off my face as I was lying in bed. Since Bob, Alan, and I were always playing cowboys and Indians. I guess I was not that surprised when Alan said, "It looks like an Indian skinned him alive." I lay as still as possible. As long as I lay still, the pain was less severe.

Three hours later, Mom came home from the hospital where she worked as a nurse. Mom looked horrified when she saw my wound. Mom yelled, "What happened?" I told her we were playing tag and I fell off the fence. Mom went in her nursing mode and took a good look at my wound. She told me my wound looked worse than it really was. Mom said we just need to keep the wound clean and free from infection. Mom gave me two aspirins for pain.

I didn't sleep much that night. Every time my arm rubbed against my wound, I would yell out in pain. The next day when Mom returned home from work, she brought some medicated gauze from the hospital. Mom gently laid the medicated gauze on my wound. Mom said, "The medicated gauze will keep the wound from getting infected." Mom told me they use the medicated gauze on burn victims.

It was six weeks before I was finally able to go outside and play "Tag You're It." Bob and Alan walked over to the fenced arena. I was reluctant to climb back on the fence. Bob and Alan said, "It's like riding a bike. When you fall off, you have to get right back on." Bob and Alan told me I had to face my fears. Alan said, "Quit being a sissy." I muttered, "I'm not a sissy."

I slowly climbed up the fence boards. I cautiously stood up on one of the fence posts. I slowly started walking across the top of the fence boards. I gained my confidence. I picked up my pace and started trotting across the top of the half-inch cedar picket fences. I stopped when I got to the gate. I turned around on the fence post. I trotted completely around the fenced arena until I reached the other side of the gate. I stopped again on the fence posts where the gate was hinged on. I recalled Bob and Alan saying I had to face my fear. I took a deep breath and thought, "Here goes." I slowly and cautiously took one step after another on top of the gate. I finally made it to the other side of the gate and rested on top of the fence post. I was proud of myself. I had faced my fears.

We played "Tag You're It" on top of the arena fence a few more times after I had been skinned alive. But Bob had made a new rule. Bob said, "When someone is crossing the gate, no one else can touch the gate. If anyone touches the gate when someone is already on it, they will automatically be 'It'."

Whenever Bob and Alan wanted to play "Tag You're It" on top of the arena fence, I found myself starting to make excuses not to play. We started moving the game "Tag You're It" over to the two-story barn. I guess I could not completely forget the pain I incurred when I was skinned alive.

CHAPTER 14

The Hunting Knife

Bob, Alan, and I were always going out to the prairie to play cowboys and Indians. Whenever we headed out to the fields, we would always take our ten-inch hunting knives. We would go exploring and search for Indian arrowheads.

It was Saturday morning in August. We still had another three weeks of freedom before school would start. Bob said, "Let's go exploring and search for some arrowheads." Alan went and got our hunting knives. Alan handed Bob and I our hunting knives. Bob stuck his hunting knife in his belt on the side of his hip. When Alan handed me my hunting knife, I told him I didn't feel like going. Alan said, "Don't be a sissy." I muttered, "I'm not a sissy." I told Alan my right side was sore and still healing from me being skinned alive. It was uncomfortable for me to wear a shirt. I told Alan and Bob I wasn't going exploring or play cowboys and Indians.

Bob and Alan headed outside to go exploring and search for arrowheads. I watched them head to the prairie from the kitchen window. I saw them crawl under the electric wire and head out toward the gully. I wished I had gone with them. I thought, "I shouldn't have let a little pain keep me from exploring, searching for arrowheads or playing cowboys and Indians."

Mike asked if I wanted to play a board game. I didn't really like playing board games. Mike always won when we played on rainy days. But I didn't have anything else to do, so I said, "Okay." Mike went into his room and came back with the board game. He was in a cheerful mood. Mike setup the game and counted out the play money for us to start with. Mike was always the banker. That was fine with me. I didn't care for all that money transactions for buying land, houses, or hotels. I just liked rolling the dice and moving my "car" token around the board. Whenever Alan and Bob played, I never got the "car" token. Alan or Bob would always pick the "car." I would usually get stuck with the dumb old "iron" token.

After about thirty minutes of playing that boring board game with Mike, I got hungry. I went to the kitchen and put two slices of bread in the toaster. When the toast popped up, I spread butter on top of the toast. I got a teaspoon and sprinkled a layer of sugar on top of the buttery toast. Finally, I got the cinnamon and sprinkled a layer of cinnamon on top of the sugar. This was my favorite breakfast. I placed the two pieces of my cinnamon sugar toast on a saucer. I returned to the living room to continue playing that boring board game. I did not offer Mike any of my delicious cinnamon sugar toast. I figured he could make his own toast. I continued playing the boring board game.

I had just about finished eating my first slice of delicious cinnamon sugar toast when I heard Bob and Alan whooping and hollering. Alan was always taking my food from me. I wasn't about for him to take my last slice of delicious cinnamon sugar toast. I slid the second slice of my delicious cinnamon sugar toast under the couch. I ran to the kitchen window. I could tell something was very wrong. Alan was crying hysterically. Bob was wide-eyed with fear. I felt a sense of panic. I have never seen my brothers act like this. As they got closer to the house, I noticed something protruding out of Bob's head.

I ran to Mike who was still sitting by the boring board game. I hollered at Mike, "Something is terribly wrong with Bob and Alan." Just about that time, Bob and Alan came crying hysterically into the house. That is when I saw what caused the horror on Bob's face.

There was a hunting knife sticking out the back of Bob's head. Mike got up and started screaming, "What happened?" Bob cried back, "I got stuck in back of the head with Alan's hunting knife." Mike told Bob to sit down on the chair. Mike said he didn't want Bob to pass out and cause more damage. Mike said he would ride his three-speed bike to the neighbor and call an ambulance. Mike told Bob not to get out of the chair. Mike told Alan and me not to let Bob get out of the chair. He said Bob might get dizzy and pass out if he gets up. Mike said Bob could fall backward and land on his head. This could drive the hunting knife further into his head which could kill him. I started to cry. Bob told me to stop crying. He said, "I'm the one that got stuck with a hunting knife." Bob said, "I won't get up out of the chair."

Mike ran to the barn and got his three-speed bike. He headed down the dirt road toward the neighbor. I never saw Mike ride that fast in all my life. It seemed like eternity before we saw Mike coming back down our dirt road. Mike was sweating and all out of breath. He said the neighbor called an ambulance and they would be here in about twenty-five minutes.

We waited about fifteen minutes. No ambulance. Bob was sitting calmly in his chair. Alan and I were fidgeting nervously. I asked Bob if it hurt. Bob replied, "No. It doesn't hurt at all." Bob said, "I'm going to try to pull it out." He reached up with both hands and tried to pull the hunting knife out of his head. The hunting knife didn't budge. Alan asked, "Did it hurt to try to pull it out?" Bob said, "No. I only feel a little pressure but it doesn't hurt."

Bob told Alan to stand on a chair and try to pull the hunting knife straight out. Alan got a chair and placed it behind Bob. He climbed on the chair and stood over Bob. Alan wrapped both hands around the handle of the hunting knife. Mike hollered, "Wait, Jeff, go get a towel in case Bob starts to bleed when the knife comes out."

Alan waited until I returned with the towel. Then Alan pulled straight up as hard as he could. The hunting knife would not budge. Alan told Mike to come help him pull out the hunting knife. Mike climbed on the chair with Alan. Mike said, "Jeff, grab Bob's shoulders and hold him down on the chair." I did what Mike instructed.

Both Mike and Alan wrapped their hands around the handle of the hunting knife. Mike said, "I will count to three and we will both pull the hunting knife straight out." When Mike said three, both Mike and Alan jerked up the hunting knife as hard as they could.

I heard a snapping sound. A snapping sound like when a small limb breaks. Mike and Alan had jerked out the hunting knife. Mike placed the hunting knife on the table. I handed the towel to Mike. Mike placed the towel on the back of Bob's head. Mike asked, "Bob, are you okay?" Bob replied, "Yes, I don't hurt at all. Did you pull the hunting knife out of my head?" Mike said, "Yes." Mike took the towel off of Bob's head. There was no blood. No blood at all. Not even one drop.

I asked Alan, "Did you hear that snapping sound?" Alan replied, "Yes." I asked Alan what that snapping sound was. Alan replied, "I don't know?" I heard it when we jerked the hunting knife out. Bob said he heard the snapping sound also. Bob picked up the hunting knife off the table. Then Bob had a bewildered look on his face. Bob said, "I think the tip of the hunting knife blade broke off in my head." Alan looked at the hunting knife. The hunting knife was missing the last half-inch tip of the blade. I don't know why but I started to cry.

About two minutes later, we heard the ambulance coming down our dirt road. The ambulance stopped in front of the house with their lights still blinking. Two men got out of the ambulance. One was carrying a red plastic box. Mike opened the door and told the men, "My brother has a hunting knife stuck in the back of his head." I heard one of the men ask Mike, "Is he still breathing?" Mike said, "Of course he is still breathing. He's sitting in the kitchen."

The two ambulance men came into the kitchen where Bob, Alan, and I were sitting at the table. One of the ambulance man asked, "Who has the hunting knife stuck in the back of his head?" Alan and I quickly pointed our finger at Bob's head. Bob said, "I'm the one who got the hunting knife stuck in the back of my head." The ambulance man carrying the red plastic box said, "Quit joking around, son. It's a serious crime to call for an ambulance when you don't need one."

Mike started yelling at the ambulance men. Mike told them they needed to get Bob to the damn emergency room right away. Alan and I were crying and telling the ambulance men Bob still had some of the knife in his head. The ambulance men saw we were all hysterical. They told us to calm down. The ambulance man with the red plastic box went over to Bob and examined the back of his head. Mike showed the other ambulance man the hunting knife. Mike told him the tip of the knife blade broke off in Bob's head when we tried to pull the knife out. The ambulance man told us we should never have tried to pull out the hunting knife ourselves. He said Bob could have bled to death. I started crying again.

The ambulance man that examined Bob's head said he saw a trace of blood on the scalp where the knife blade had entered his scalp. He then got real serious. He knew we were not joking. He ordered the other ambulance man to go get the gurney. The other ambulance man went to the ambulance and retrieved a flat board. The ambulance man told Bob to lie on his stomach on the board. Bob started arguing with the men. He said he could walk to the ambulance. The ambulance men would have no part of it. They said Bob could get dizzy and pass out. After Bob lay down on his stomach on the board, the ambulance men picked up the board. They carried Bob out to ambulance and slid him in the back of the vehicle. The ambulance men told us they were taking him to the hospital emergency room. They turned on the siren and sped away.

After the ambulance was out of sight, Alan and I went to the kitchen and sat down at the table. I asked Alan what happened. Alan started sobbing and said, "It was an accident." Alan said, "We didn't get half way to the gullies when I tripped over a log." Alan said they decided to practice throwing their hunting knives into the log. Bob walked to the log. He paced off ten-long strides away from the log. Bob drew a line in the ground with his hunting knife. Bob said we couldn't step across the line when throwing the hunting knife toward the log.

Alan said they had been throwing their hunting knives and hitting their target. The hunting knives were sticking in the log. Alan said, "We both would go up to the log at the same time to retrieve our hunting knives." After about throwing the hunting knives about five minutes, Alan said he threw his hunting knife and it missed the target. His knife sailed over the log and landed about ten feet past the log. Bob's hunting knife hit the target solid. Bob went to the log and pulled out his hunting knife. Alan kept on walking to where his hunting knife landed in the dirt. Bob walked back to the throwing line. He threw his knife at the log and hit his target squarely.

Alan said he was returning to the throwing line when he passed Bob going to the log to retrieve his hunting knife. Alan said he was pretending a rattlesnake was going to strike Bob. Alan said he threw his hunting knife quickly and hard to kill the make-believe rattlesnake. Alan said he missed the make-believe rattlesnake. The hunting knife sailed to the left toward Bob. Alan said he screamed at Bob to duck. But it was too late. Bob jerked out his hunting knife out of the log. As Bob jerked his head upward, Alan's hunting knife was coming down and struck Bob squarely on the back of the head.

Alan said Bob yelled out in pain. Bob turned around and asked Alan why he hit him on the back of the head. Bob said it felt like he got hit with a baseball bat. Alan said he just started crying hysterically. Alan said they tried to pull the knife out but was unable to budge it. Then they ran home with the hunting knife sticking straight out of Bob's head.

Mom worked at the hospital where they took Bob. The doctors told Mom her son Bob had been stuck in the back of the head with a hunting knife. The doctor told Mom the knife blade had broken off and was still wedged in his skull. The doctor had said the knife blade was millimeters from his brain. The doctor said it was a miracle the hunting knife blade broke off. He said Bob may have bled to death if the entire knife blade came out. The doctor said it was too dangerous to operate because the knife blade was so close to the brain. The doctor said all his neurology tests were normal. But they were going to keep Bob overnight to monitor him.

When Mom came home that night, she looked exhausted. Mike, Alan, and I all asked Mom at the same time if Bob was going to be okay. Mom said, "It's a miracle Bob's alive, but he will be okay." She told us the doctors were keeping him overnight for observations.

The next evening, Bob came home with Mom from the hospital. Alan and I asked Bob how he felt. Bob said, "I feel great." Bob told us how cool it was to ride in the ambulance to the hospital. Bob said, "The sirens were blaring and we were speeding fast. It was really cool."

A month later, we were playing "tag you're it," exploring, searching for arrowheads, and playing cowboys and Indians. This one Saturday, we were heading out to play like usual. Mom stopped us at the door. Mom said, "You boys are going to clean the entire house before you boys go and play." I got the luxury of cleaning the living room. I had to vacuum the entire floor. That meant vacuuming behind the furniture. As I moved the couch, I saw a slice of old cinnamon sugar toast on a saucer. I remembered in horror how I shoved that piece of toast under the couch so Alan wouldn't eat it. I remembered Bob and Alan running into the house screaming and hollering. I remembered seeing the huge hunting knife sticking out of Bob's head like it was just yesterday. I threw the toast in the garbage and washed the saucer. I guess I will never forget the day Bob got stuck in the back of the head with Alan's hunting knife.

CHAPTER 15

The Broken Arm

It was a nice fall weekend in September and the year was 1962. As usual, Bob, Alan, and I were getting ready to play "Tag You're It" out in the barn. Since Mike never came out and played with us, I thought it would be nice to have him play with us. I asked, "Mike, come out and play 'Tag You're It' with us." He replied, "No, I have homework to do." I told Mike it was the weekend and he could do his homework Sunday. He just stated, "I have enough homework to keep me busy for both Saturday and Sunday." I pleaded with Mike to come outside and play "Tag You're It." I told Mike, "We play board games with you on rainy days but you never play outside with us." I begged Mike, "Come on and play 'Tag You're It' just one time." Mike reluctantly agreed to come outside and play "Tag You're It." But Mike said we would have to play a board game when we were done playing "Tag You're It." I promised, "Okay we will play your board game."

We ran out to the barn to play "Tag You're It." I showed Mike the interior of the barn. The barn was two stories high. The barn was about seventy feet long and thirty feet wide. The barn had two floor ledges ten feet high from the ground floor. The floor ledges were ten feet wide on both the left and right side of the barn. There was about fifteen feet of open space on the second floor. There were wooden ladders attached to both ledges at the back of the barn. There was a four-inch-wide wooden beam running the length of the back wall from one ledge to the other ledge. There was an iron rail on the front side of the barn. The iron rail ran the length of the front side of the barn from ledge to ledge. The barn consisted of six support beams from ground floor to the roof. Three of the support beams were on the left side of the barn and three of the support beams were on the right side of the barn.

Bob explained the rules for playing "Tag You're It" when in the barn. Bob told Mike we drew sticks to see who would be "It" first. Whoever drew the shortest stick would be "It" first. Bob told Mike whoever was "It" first would have to count to fifty. This would give everyone else a head start to get away. I showed Mike the middle support beam on the left side of the barn. I told Mike you were safe when you were touching that support beam. That way you could rest a little and catch your breath. No one could tag you if you were touching that beam.

I pointed to where Mike would have to cross the four-inch wooded beam at the back of the barn to cross from one ledge to the other ledge. I showed Mike he would have to crawl hand over hand on the steel rail at the front of the barn to cross from one ledge to the other ledge. I told Mike if you dropped down to the ground floor, you were automatically "It." After explaining the rules to Mike, we were ready to start playing "Tag You're It."

We all climbed up the wooden ladder on the left side of the barn to the second story ledge. Bob picked up four sticks and held them with both hands hiding the length of the sticks. He told Mike to draw first since this was the first time he was playing "Tag You're It" with us. Mike drew a long stick. Alan drew second. Alan drew a shorter stick than Mike. I drew a longer stick than Alan's stick. Bob looked at his remaining stick and it was longer than Alan's stick. The ritual was over. Alan was first to be "It."

Alan started counting as fast as he could to fifty. I ran to the back of the barn with Mike following me. I ran across the four-inch wooden beam to the ledge on the other side of the barn. Mike was a little nervous. Mike walked cautiously across the four-inch wooden beam to the other ledge. Just as Mike had reached the ledge on the right side of the barn, Alan came running as fast as he could after Mike.

I was laughing and really happy Mike finally came outside to play with us. I was running to the front side of the barn. I swung down hanging onto the iron rail. I kicked my feet up and wrapped them over the iron rail. I then crawled hand over hand on the iron rail crossing to the ledge on the other side of the barn. When I reached the other side, I unwrapped my feet from the iron rail and dropped down to the second story ledge.

I looked back and saw Mike staring at the iron rail. I yelled at Mike to hurry up. I hollered, "Alan's going to catch you." I told Mike to grab the iron rail and wrap his feet around the iron rail like I did. Mike grabbed the iron rail with his hands with his feet dangling in air. I hollered at Mike to wrap his feet around the rail and cross over hand over hand. Mike swung his feet up and wrapped them over the iron rail. Mike started scooting over the rail hand over hand. Mike had taken too long to start crossing the iron rail. Alan was catching up. I hollered at Mike to hurry or Alan was going to catch him.

Mike tried to scoot over the iron rail faster. Mike got halfway from one ledge to the other ledge when everything went wrong. Mike's hand slipped off the iron rail. Mike lost his grip and fell hard fourteen feet to the ground floor. Mike landed awkwardly on his right arm. Mike screamed out in agony as the bone in his right arm broke through the skin. Mike lay on his side in a crumple heap.

Bob, Alan, and I all jumped to the ground floor to help Mike. Bob and Alan helped Mike up to his feet. Bob instructed Alan and I to get Mike to the house. Bob ran to his three-speed bike and rode to the neighbor to call the ambulance. When we got Mike to the house, we told him to lie down on the couch and wait for the ambulance. The ambulance arrived at the house the same time Bob returned from the neighbor. I guess the ambulance were getting familiar with our address. They seemed to be getting to our house quicker.

The ambulance man took one look at Mike's arm and immediately escorted him to the ambulance. The ambulance man said Mike would be okay. They were taking him to the emergency room so the doctor could fix his arm. They sped off with sirens blaring and lights flashing.

After the ambulance left, Bob, Alan, and I sat on the couch and breathed a sigh of relief. Alan said, "Did you see the way that bone stuck out of his skin?" I got nausea just thinking about it and nearly threw up. Bob reassured us that Mike would be okay. Bob told us they have very good doctors at the hospital. After all, that's where they took him when he had the hunting knife stuck in the back of his head.

Mike returned home with Mom from the hospital. Mom looked weary and very tired. Mike had a white cast on his arm from his elbow to his hand. Only his fingers and thumb were sticking out of the cast. I asked Mike if his arm still hurt. He said it hurt a little but he was okay. He said the doctor gave him some pain medication and then fixed the broken arm. Alan went and got a pen and said he wanted to sign his name on Mike's cast. Alan signed his name. Bob signed his name. I was last to sign my name on the cast. After I signed my name, I wrote "Tag You're It." We all laughed at that. I thought to myself, the first time we get Mike to come outside and play with us, he falls and breaks his arm. I guess we will have to play board games with him for quite some time.

CHAPTER 16

The Dog

It was Bob who spotted the dog on the side of the road in a ditch. Dad, Bob and I were driving home from the hardware store. Bob was riding shotgun (in the front passenger seat). I was sitting in the back-seat behind Bob. Bob saw the dog lying in the ditch as we passed by. Bob yelled at Dad telling him there was an injured dog in the ditch. Dad slammed on the brakes and backed up. Dad and Bob got out of the car and walked over to the injured dog in the ditch. Dad told Bob to stay back. Dad said injured dogs can bite anyone who tries to help them.

Dad looked the injured dog over talking softly to her. Dad saw the dog had tangled herself up with a rope made of twine. The rope twine was used to bind bales of hay. The twine was tangled tightly around the dog. The twine wrapped around both hind legs, around the right front paw and tightly around her neck. The twine wrapped around her hind legs were so tight it cut through the skin to the bone. The twine around her neck was so tight it was choking her. Dad said it was a good thing they came by. Dad said the dog would not have lived much longer.

Dad soothed the dog and patted the dog on the head. Dad got out his pocket knife and carefully cut the twine around the dog's neck. As soon as the twine was cut, the dog whimpered and started breathing better. Then Dad took the pocket knife and carefully cut the twine wrapping the hind legs. Dad could not cut the twine wrapped around the hind legs without cutting some more skin. Dad kept talking soothingly to the dog as he gently cut the twine. The dog kept nibbling at Dad's hands as he cut the twine. The dog seemed to know Dad was trying to help her. After Dad cut the twine off the dog's hind legs, he was able to unwrap the twine from the front paw.

Dad picked the dog up gently in his arms and carried her out of the ditch to the car. I scooted to the left side of the car seat. Dad placed the dog in the backseat. Bob climbed in the backseat and held the dog's head in his lap. Bob rubbed the dog's head gently as Dad drove home.

Dad carried the dog into the house. Dad told Alan to go warm up some milk for the dog. Dad told me to go get a blanket and fold it up on the floor. I went a got a blanket. I folded the blanket up and laid it on the couch. I thought the dog needed a softer bed than the floor. Dad said nothing and placed the injured dog on top of the blanket on the couch. Alan held the bowl of warm milk in front of the dog's mouth. The dog lapped up the warm milk and then went to sleep.

Mike, Bob, Alan, and I nursed the dog back to health. We never left the dog alone for the next three days. One of us was always with the dog. We were either giving her warm milk, putting salve on her cuts, or petting her gently. About a week later, the dog was able to start walking around the house with us. The dog never left our side.

After the dog was almost fully recovered from her injuries, Dad told us boys to sit at the table. Usually when we all had to sit at the table, it was bad news. Dad said, "If the dog's owner comes for her, we will have to give her back." Bob shouted, "The dog was abused and ran away from her owner." Dad said, "We don't know that for sure." Dad said, "I will post a sign in town, we have a lost dog. If no one claims the dog after one month, we will keep her." Dad said, "I don't believe anyone will claim the dog." Dad said the dog was not a registered breed dog. The dog is a mixed breed. The dog looks like she is part golden retriever, part cocker spaniel and part 57 Heinz. I asked Dad, "What's a 57 Heinz dog?" Dad just said that it could be any mixture breed dog. That did not make sense to me. I thought the dog was a pure bred dog. I knew one thing for sure, she was a very smart dog.

Dad told us we should not give her a name. Dad said it might confuse her if the owner gave her a different name. Dad told us we could give her a name after one month because then we would keep her. We all realized the dog was living with us for about a week now with no name. Bob said, "Her hair is the same color as sand." Bob told us it was a miracle he saw her in the ditch. Her hair matched the color of the road. Bob said, "We should name her Sandy." Mike, Alan, and I all agreed. We would name her Sandy in one month. Only, we did not wait a month to name her Sandy. We started calling her Sandy immediately. Like I said, Sandy was a very smart dog. Sandy immediately responded to her new name.

That month was one of our longest months ever. Finally, Bob told Dad it had been one month. Bob asked, "Sandy is our dog now, right?" Dad replied, "Yes, the dog belongs to us."

Since we never left Sandy's side when she was injured, she never left our side when we went exploring or playing cowboys and Indians. One morning, Bob, Alan, and I went on an exploring trip to hunt for Indian arrow heads. Whenever we went exploring, we would take our hunting knives and our walking sticks. As usual, Sandy was right by our side. We headed out toward the prairie.

We had walked about five miles when we came to a two-lane paved road. On the other side of the paved road was a huge cattle pasture. There were three galvanized steel tanks scattered throughout the pasture. The galvanized steel tanks were used to hold water for the cattle. Bob said, "That looks like our new swimming pool." We crossed the paved road and climbed through the fence. Sandy followed right by our side. Sandy crouched down and crawled under the barbed wire as I pulled the wire up. We went to one of the galvanized steel tanks. It was about three feet high. It had about four inches of water. It was not deep enough to go swimming in. Bob said, "The tanks will fill up with water after a storm. We will go swimming after a storm moves through." Sounded good to me.

We continued exploring. We had heard there was a sandpit somewhere around here. But we had no idea where it was. We continued walking. Alan was walking out in front. Bob was walking about two feet behind. And like usual, I was bringing up the rear. All of a sudden, Sandy darted in front of Alan. Sandy snatched a snake and threw it in the air away from Alan. Bob, Alan, and I walked to where Sandy had thrown the snake. We took our walking sticks and commenced beating that snake to death. Sandy gave a growl toward us as if to say, "Stay behind me."

From that moment on, Sandy took the lead and we followed her. She seemed to know where we wanted to go. About forty-five minutes later, we came to the sandpit we had heard about. It was a huge sandpit. Bob pointed to a nest in the side of the cliff. Bob said it looked like an eagle's nest. We got all excited and started climbing toward the eagle's nest.

When we finally got to the nest, we discovered it was not an eagle's nest but instead an owl's nest. The owl's nest had three baby owls squeaking. Bob said, "Once a bird smells humans in their nest, they will abandon their babies." Bob said we would have to take the babies and feed them ourselves so they can live. Alan took off his shirt. Alan made the shirt into a pouch. We placed the three baby owls in the shirt pouch and climbed down the side of the cliff.

When we got to the ground, Sandy sniffed at the three baby owls and started wagging her tail in approval. I got the honor of carrying the baby owls home. I was careful not to drop them. Sandy was keeping an eye on me also to make sure I wouldn't drop them.

When we got home with the owls, Bob got a big box. We placed the box in the storage shed. We placed straw on the bottom of the box so the owls would think it was their nest. We dug up some earthworms and fed the three baby owls. The baby owls seemed to be starving because they swallowed those earthworms whole. We fed the baby owls earthworms every day.

After about a week, we found out the hard way. There is a reason why a mother bird eats the food first, digests the food, and then throws up the food into the baby's open mouth. A baby owl cannot digest earthworms. The earthworms were eating their way out of the baby owl's stomach. The earthworms were coming out of the baby's owl's eyes.

Bob told Alan and me we had to put the owls out of their misery. I started to cry. I could not bring myself to put my owl out of its misery. Alan said, "If I didn't put the owl out of its misery, it would suffer until it died. It could suffer for another month." Sandy licked my hand. Sandy knew I was upset. I told Alan I couldn't do it. Bob said he would take care of it for me. Bob told me to take Sandy to the house. Bob told me to get a newspaper so we could bury the owls.

I took Sandy to the house. I returned back to the storage shed with a newspaper. Bob told me that this was part of life. We each took a newspaper page and wrapped our dead baby owls. Bob dug a shallow grave behind the storage shed. We placed the dead baby owls in the grave side by side. We covered the grave with the dirt. We placed a little cross for each owl. I thought, "Life isn't always fair. Life is what it is."

A couple weeks later, a big thunderstorm came through Kansas. The next day Bob, Alan, and I headed to our swimming pool in the cattle pasture. Sandy was leading the way. It was like she knew exactly where we were going. When we got to the cattle pasture we climbed through the barbed wire. Sandy crouched down and crawled under while I pulled up the barbed wire. She was getting good at this. Sandy led the way to the swimming pool (galvanized steel tanks).

We were about fifty feet from our swimming pool when Sandy stopped abruptly. The hair on the back of her neck stood straight up and she was growling. We knew this was another snake. We walked around where the snake was and called for Sandy to come on. She ran over to us and started leading the way again toward the swimming pool.

The galvanized steel tank was about three-fourths full of water from the rain storm. We tore off our clothes except for our underwear. We jumped into the tank. Sandy walked about ten feet away and came running full speed toward the tank. She leaped in the air and landed in our swimming pool. We splashed and played for hours in the galvanized water tank. That was the best day of my life.

Every time a thunderstorm moved through the area, Bob, Alan, and I would head to our swimming pool. Sandy would always lead the way keeping us out of danger from the snakes. One time, we were walking to our swimming pool. We had not even made it to the two-lane paved road. Sandy started barking and running around in circles. Every once in a while, she would jump up in the air. She wasn't warning us of danger. The hair on the back of her neck would stand straight up when we were in danger. This was not the case. It looked like she was in a playful mood.

We walked over to where Sandy was barking and jumping around playfully. We saw a nest in the ground. There were three baby rabbits in the nest. Sandy started licking the baby rabbits. We always seemed to find animals in sets of three. One for Bob, one for Alan, and one for me. Bob said, "The mother rabbit must be dead. They would never leave their babies alone. We'll take them home and take care of them."

I said, "I'm not going to feed them earthworms." Bob said, "No, we will feed them rabbit food." We turned around and took the baby rabbits home. Like with the baby owls, we got a big box and placed straw on the bottom. We made a nice nest for the baby rabbits. Unlike the baby owls, these baby rabbits grew up big and strong. We took the grown rabbits back to the place where we found them and let them go.

Then one day, we came back from our trip to the cattle pasture. We had a fun-filled day of swimming in our galvanized water tank. Dad was sitting at the kitchen table. Dad said, "Boys, sit down at the table." I knew this was going to be bad news. Dad said, "A man told me he saw three boys playing in a cattle pasture swimming in the water tanks." Dad asked, "Was those three boys you boys?" We all said, "Yes, sir." Bob said, "We swim in the cattle's water tank after it rains."

Dad said, "The man that saw you boys told me that pasture was called Rattlesnake Pasture because of all the rattlesnakes. They don't keep cattle in there anymore because the rattlesnakes were killing so many of the cattle." Alan said, "That's okay, Sandy protects us. She lets us know where the snakes are and we walk around them."

I added, "Yeah, Sandy threw a snake up in the air away from Alan when he almost stepped on it." I should never had added that remark.

Dad yelled, "You mean you boys were aware of the rattlesnakes in the pasture and you still kept going? What in the hell is wrong with you, boys?" Dad said, "From this day on, you boys are not to set foot in Rattlesnake Pasture, do you understand?" We all said, "Yes, sir." Although, I really didn't understand why we couldn't go to our swimming pool. We told Dad Sandy always protected us.

Then one day, the unthinkable happened. Mike was riding his bike to school. Sandy had escorted Alan and me to the school bus. Since Mike was riding his bike to school, Sandy continued to trot behind Mike. I waved at Mike as the school bus passed him by. On the way home from school, the school bus would usually pass Mike riding the bike. This afternoon I did not see the school bus passing Mike.

The school bus dropped us off at the end of our driveway. Sandy was usually waiting for us to get off the school bus. Sandy was nowhere around. I hollered out for Sandy. No Sandy. Alan and I walked the half mile dirt driveway to our farmhouse. I walked into the house calling for Sandy. No Sandy. No one was at home.

It was late when Dad came home. Dad was carrying Sandy in his arms. Dad laid Sandy on the couch the same way he did when we first got her. Sandy was in a cast from her hip to her hind legs. I ran to Sandy and started petting her on the head.

Dad said, "Sandy had been hit by a car." Dad said, "She broke her hip and both hind legs." We nursed Sandy back to health like we did when we first got her. We never left her side. About six weeks later, the cast was removed. Sandy's back hind quarters were crooked. She never walked the same after her car accident. Sandy couldn't run around like she used to. Sandy's health wouldn't allow her to follow us on our exploration trips anymore. Sandy was now just a house dog. When I got back home from playing cowboys and Indians or exploring for Indian arrow heads, I would always go give Sandy a hug and play with her awhile.

Sandy only lived about six months after the car accident. We were all very sad. I loved that dog. I cried as we buried her behind the storage shed. Bob hammered in a wooden cross by her grave. On the wooden cross it said, "We Love You Sandy." Again, I realized that life isn't fair. Life is what it is. Everyone leaves you sooner or later. You have to pick yourself up, be strong and rely on no one but yourself.

CHAPTER 17

The Last Slice of Pie

Mike, my oldest brother, had broken his arm two weeks ago. Bob had a hunting knife stuck in his head a month or so earlier. I had been skinned alive about three months ago. I guess we had a run of bad luck. But our luck was about to change. Dad had just started a new job at the quarry sand pit. Mom decided we deserved a fine cooked meal topped off with a cherry pie.

It was the first Thursday in October. Mom did not have to work at the hospital that night. Mom made a delicious meal. And for dessert, Mom made my favorite cherry pie. I probably could eat a whole cherry pie all by myself. I said probably. Whenever there was a pie on the table, my brothers would all dig in and I would get what was left over.

Mom made meatloaf, mashed potatoes, gravy, and corn on the cob. Again, like I said, she made my favorite cherry pie for dessert. We all ate like pigs. I meant to say like hungry boys. Mom cut the cherry pie into slices. She gave each of us a slice of cherry pie on a saucer. There was one slice of cherry pie left in the pie pan. Mom looked at all of us and sternly said, "That last slice of pie is for your father's lunch tomorrow." Mom said, "Your father has been working very hard at his new job and deserves a slice of cherry pie."

Mom made Alan and I clean the dirty dishes. While Alan and I were taking the dirty dishes to the sink, Mom wrapped up the last slice of cherry pie in the pie pan with plastic wrap. When Alan and I finished washing and drying the dishes we headed to our bedroom. As I walked past the table, I saw the last slice of cherry pie wrapped up in the pie pan. I couldn't help but lick my lips. You could see right through that clear plastic wrap. That cherry pie looked mighty delicious. I was jealous that Dad was going to get to eat that last slice of cherry pie. I walked reluctantly to my bedroom.

I finally dozed off and went to sleep. About three thirty in the morning, I woke up really thirsty. I got out of bed and walked to the kitchen to get a drink of water. As I passed the table, I saw the last slice of cherry pie still wrapped up in the pie pan. I could not believe Dad did not eat that piece of cherry pie when he got home from work. I kept walking to the sink. I got a glass from the counter top and poured me a glass of water. I drank the water and started walking back to the bedroom.

As I passed the table, I glanced at the last slice of cherry pie wrapped in the pie pan. I took two steps toward the hall. I should not have glanced at the last slice of cherry pie. I turned around and stood over the cherry pie. I started thinking. You are going to be in big trouble if you eat that last slice of cherry pie. Dad is going to give you a good spanking. I started licking my lips. I began to rationalize that Dad must not really want that cherry pie. Otherwise, he would have eaten it last night when he got home from work. Then I remembered Mom telling all of us the last slice of pie was off limits. That it was for Dad's lunch at work.

I thought, "I'll just get a small sliver of that cherry pie. No one will even notice." I walked over to the drawer and quietly pulled out a fork. I quietly unwrapped the plastic wrap covering the last slice of cherry pie. I took the fork and with the fork prongs, I carefully cut a small sliver of cherry pie. I ate the small sliver of cherry pie. I thought, "Damn, that was a delicious cherry pie." You couldn't even tell I took a sliver of pie. So I took another sliver of cherry pie. Then one more sliver of cherry pie. I should never had taken that third sliver of cherry pie. I looked at the last slice of cherry pie. I thought,

"I'm in big trouble." That was one puny slice of cherry pie left in the pie dish. So I convinced myself, if I was going to be in big trouble anyway, I may as well enjoy the rest of that delicious cherry pie. So I ate the last slice of cherry pie. I walked to my bedroom. I didn't even have the decency to put the empty pie dish in the sink.

At 6:30 a.m., our bedroom door was jerked opened. Dad yelled, "Get to the kitchen now." I knew when Dad yelled in that voice, you better mind him. Alan and I scrambled out of bed and ran to the kitchen. Bob and Mike was already standing at the table where that empty pie dish was sitting on the table. I thought, "Uh, oh, I'm in big trouble now." Dad yelled, "Who ate the last slice of pie?" It was self-preservation as I was the first to yell, "Not me." All my other brothers followed saying, "Not me, not me, and not me."

Dad said, "I'm going to ask each of you one more time." Dad looked directly at Mike and asked, "Did you eat the last piece of pie?" Mike replied, "No, sir." Dad looked directly at Bob and asked the same question. Bob replied, "No, sir." Dad looked directly at Alan and asked him. Alan replied, "No, sir." Finally, it was my turn. Dad looked me directly in my eyes. Dad asked, "Did you eat the last slice of pie?" I stammered. I wanted to confess and say honestly, "Yes, sir." But "No, sir" came out of my shaky voice. Dad yelled, "Someone sure as hell ate the last slice of pie." Dad said, "I have to go to work now. But I'll get to the bottom of this when I get home tonight."

After Dad went to work, I walked back to my bedroom. I crawled into bed and was feeling miserable for lying. I was getting sick at my stomach. I lay in bed wishing I had not lied when Dad asked who ate the last slice of pie. Then I got to thinking. Maybe I didn't really tell a lie. Dad had asked, "Who ate the last slice of pie?" Dad did not ask, "Who ate the last slice of cherry pie?" Dad could have been talking about another pie. I still had a miserable day. I stayed in my bedroom the entire day playing with my toy cars. But I was not having any fun. I was dreading when Dad would come home from work. I remembered Dad said he was going to get to the bottom of who ate the last slice of pie.

I was glad when it was time to go to bed. It had been a long miserable day for me. I was dreading when Dad would get home. I figured Dad would yell at us to get to the kitchen so he could interrogate us again. Fortunately for me, Dad had to work late that day. He didn't come home until way after dark. I didn't even hear Dad come home. In fact, I was startled when Dad woke us up the next morning.

Dad seemed to be in a good mood. Dad said, "Get dressed and go to the living room." I thought, "Uh, oh, we're going to get interrogated." Alan and I got dressed. I nervously followed Alan into the living room. Mike and Bob were already sitting on the couch. Alan sat by Bob and I sat by Alan. Dad asked cheerfully, "Would you boys like to go to Dodge City and visit Boot Hill today?" Now, Bob, Alan, and I were always playing cowboys and Indians. Who wouldn't want to go to Dodge City where Wyatt Earp was the U.S. Marshal. And to go to Boot Hill where Wyatt Earp killed all the bad guys and buried them there. We all jumped up and down except for Mike, and yelled, "Heck yeah."

Dad said, "Are you sure you want to go to Boot Hill?" We all screamed excitedly at Dad and said, "Heck, yeah." Dad said, "Okay, then we will go as soon as someone tells me who ate the last slice of pie." I felt a wave of panic flow through me. I thought, "That damn slice of pie." Dad just stood there waiting for someone to answer. No one admitted eating the last slice of pie. Dad said, "Okay, I guess you boys will not be going to Boot Hill."

Bob finally said, "Dad, let me talk to Mike, Alan, and Jeff to see if we can figure out who ate the last slice of pie." To my surprise, Dad said, "Okay." Dad left the living room. He walked to the kitchen and got him a cup of coffee. When we were by ourselves, Bob said, "Let's all swear on the bible to tell the truth." That way, we will find out who ate the last slice of pie. Mike said, "It's not right to swear on the bible." I said, "Yeah, Mike's the smart one, we should listen to him." Bob thought for a few minutes then said, "Okay, we will draw straws. If you did not eat the last slice of pie, God will not let you draw the short straw." Mike and Alan said, "Okay, that sounds fair." I couldn't think of an argument, so I said okay. I thought, "I'm going to get caught in my lie now."

Bob went outside and got four sticks. Bob broke one of the sticks a little shorter than the rest of them. Bob came into the house and handed the sticks to Mike. Bob said, "We will let Jeff draw first, then Alan and then I'll draw. Mike will have the stick that is left over." We all agreed. I just knew I was going to draw the shortest stick. After all, Bob said God would not let someone draw the short straw if they did not eat the last slice of pie. I nervously drew my stick from Mike's hand. I looked at my stick. It looked pretty short to me. Then Alan drew a stick from Mike's hand. He placed his stick next to my stick. Alan's stick was longer than my stick. Alan said, "Yes, I knew I didn't eat the last slice of pie. I'm in the clear." Then Bob drew a stick from Mike's hand. Bob's stick looked pretty short. Bob compared his stick to Mike's stick. Mike's stick was longer than Bob's. Mike was in the clear. Since Alan's stick was longer than my stick, Bob compared his stick with my stick. Bob's stick was a good two inches shorter than mine. Bob took a double look at his stick. Bob had a look of shock on his face. There was no way he should have gotten the shortest stick. I shouted out, "Yeah, I'm in the clear."

Bob still in disbelief said, "I know for a fact that I did not eat that last slice of pie." Bob said, "God knows I did not eat the last slice of pie. But I will tell Dad I ate the last slice of pie so we can go to Boot Hill." Bob walked to the kitchen and told Dad he ate the last slice of pie.

Dad told Bob to bend over the chair. Dad said he was spanking him for lying to him and not for eating the last slice of pie. Dad gave Bob four whacks on the butt with his belt. Bob did not cry. I felt bad. Bob was taking a whipping that I should be getting. After Dad finished spanking Bob, he came into the living room and sat us all down on the couch. Dad said, "Never lie. You are a Tracey. Traceys are honest and hardworking. Never forget that."

Then Dad said, "Okay, go get into the car. We're going to Boot Hill." Mike, Bob, and Alan jumped up excitedly and ran to the car. Ridden with guilt, I followed them slowly to the car. Alan yelled at me to hurry up and get in the car. I was completely quiet the entire trip to Dodge City.

At Boot Hill, Bob and Alan were running all over the place having a great time. Even Mike seemed to be having fun. There were cowboys walking around Boot Hill. The cowboys even put on a gunfight show for the crowd. I couldn't shake the feeling of being miserable. All I could think about was Bob getting a spanking for something I did. I made up my mind I would not tell another lie. Dad finally told us it was time to go home.

On the way back home, I was sitting between Bob and Alan in the backseat. We were almost home when I blurted out, "Dad, I was the one who ate the last slice of cherry pie. Not Bob." Dad said, "I know. I heard your bedroom door open in the middle of the night." I was shocked with disbelief. I asked Dad, "Why did you spank Bob when you knew I ate the last slice of cherry pie." Dad replied, "Bob lied when he told me he ate the last slice of pie. He got spanked for lying." Then Dad said, "And you are going to get a spanking for lying when we get home." I said, "Okay." I was glad I finally told the truth. It felt like a heavy weight was lifted off of me.

We finally drove up to the house. Bob exited the car. I followed Bob. As I stood up, Bob punched me in the stomach. I doubled over in pain. Bob said, "That's for letting me take the blame for eating the last slice of pie." I told Bob I was very sorry. Dad kept his word. When we walked in the house, Dad told me to bend over the same chair he had Bob bend over. Dad spanked me eight times with the belt. And I cried. I guess Dad gave me four of Bob's whacks. But I was not feeling miserable anymore. I vowed not to lie anymore. Lying was just not worth it. And I was not very good at it. Next time if I am told not to eat the last slice of cherry pie or any pie, I will not eat the last slice of pie. That is for sure.

CHAPTER 18

The Horrible Accident

A cold front had just moved through the last week in October 1962. My dad had just started a new job. He was working at a quarry sand-pit. He loaded rocks and small boulders into a large auger. The auger had two large blades that worked together pulling the rocks and small boulders into a large grinder. The large grinder would break up the rocks and small boulders into gravel. The gravel was used for maintaining county roads in Kansas.

The sun had just set and darkness was covering the quarry sand-pit. Dad had just dumped a load of rocks and small boulders onto the large auger. About two minutes later, the large grinder started shaking and shuttering. Dad got off his tractor and walked over to the large grinder. He saw a couple of boulders were jamming the large grinders.

Dad picked up the large iron pole used to push one of the small boulders away from the grinder. As he pushed one of the boulders away from the grinder, he slipped forward. The large grinder stopped shaking and shuttering. It immediately pulled the small boulder and rocks into the grinder.

When Dad slipped forward, the flap of his overcoat got caught in the large grinder. It pulled him toward the large grinder. Dad used both hands and pushed backward as hard as he could. Dad screamed to the man at the control switch to hit the emergency shut-off button. Since the darkness had covered the quarry sandpit, the man at the control switch did not see what was happening to my dad. The Kansas prairie wind was also howling that night. The man at the control switch did not hear Dad's screaming for him to hit the emergency shut-off button.

The large grinder continued to pull Dad toward the deadly steel teeth. Dad shoved the small boulder that he had dislodged earlier in front of his chest. The small boulder was crushed into fine gravel. Dad continued to scream to the man at the control switch to hit the emergency shut-off button. The large grinder shredded Dad's overcoat he was wearing. The large grinder shredded the sweater Dad was wearing. The large grinder shredded the shirt Dad was wearing. Dad said he prayed for the man to hit the emergency shut-off button. The grinder started shredding the skin on Dad's chest. Dad was pushing backward with all his might. He was no match for the mighty steel grinder. Just as the steel grinder was about to shred Dad's heart, the steel grinder stopped. Dad was on the verge of losing conscious but fought to stay awake.

The man at the control switch later told Dad he never saw what was happening because of the darkness. He said all he could hear was the Kansas howling wind. The man at the control switch told Dad an eerie voice from the howling wind told him to hit the shut-off button. The man hit the emergency shut-off button immediately. When the auger and large grinder stopped immediately, he said he could hear Dad's screaming. The man took his flashlight and saw Dad halfway in the grinder. He immediately put the grinder in reverse mode. The iron grinder released the deadly hold he had on my dad's chest. My dad fell backward in a heap.

The man at the control switch called an ambulance and ran to help my dad. He pulled Dad off the auger and laid him on the ground. When he saw Dad's chest, he had to look away. He thought Dad was going to die. The ambulance men came within fifteen minutes. The ambulance men checked out Dad. They also looked away and thought Dad was going to die. They immediately put him on the gurney and carried him to the ambulance. The man at the control switch said he would pray for my dad as the ambulance sped away.

It was about 10:00 p.m. when Mom woke up Mike, Bob, Alan, and me. There was a police officer in our living room. I could see the police car blinking lights out the front door. Mom told us Dad was in a horrible accident. Mom told us the police officer was going to take us to the hospital. Mike said, "Let us get dressed." Mom replied, "There is no time." We got in the police car wearing our pajamas.

The police officer turned on the siren and kept the lights blinking. The police officer was flying down the gravel roads. I never knew a car could move so fast. Before we knew it, we were pulling up at the emergency entrance. The police officer escorted us into the hospital. I was starting to get scared. Bob asked Mom what was going on. Mom said, "Your dad was in a horrible accident, and he may not live through the night." I started to cry.

The police officer instructed Mom and us kids to wait in the waiting room. A few minutes later, a nurse came into the waiting room. The nurse told Mom that Dad was in critical condition. She said they had to call in a heart specialist to operate on him. The nurse told us we could see Dad after his surgery was completed. The nurse told Mom she would take care of Dad and let him know we were all here.

Dad was in an ER waiting for a heart specialist to arrive at the hospital and operate. Dad had an IV hooked up to him on his arm. The nurse returned to Dad. The nurse replaced Dad's IV bag and wiped his forehead with a damp rag. She told Dad that we were all at the hospital and in the waiting room.

Dad told the nurse to go get us. He wanted to see his family right now. The nurse told Dad, "No way. You have an open wound and we have to keep you isolated." Dad angrily said, "I want to see my family right now. If you don't bring my family to me, then I will go to my family." Dad sat up on the edge of the bed. Dad pulled out the IV from his arm. The nurse hollered at two male nurse assistance to hold Dad down. Dad fought them fiercely trying to get up. Dad's chest started to bleed from his exertion. The nurse gave up. She told Dad to lie back down on the bed. The nurse said she would let the family come visit him after she hooked the IV back in his arm. Dad stopped fighting and let the nurse insert the IV back in his arm. The nurse left Dad to come get us.

The nurse walked into the waiting room shaking her head. She told Mom what had happened with Dad. She told Mom we could only visit for five minutes then we had to leave. She told Mom that Dad had an open wound and infection could set in. Mom promised we would leave after five minutes.

Mom followed the nurse to where Dad was at. Mike, Bob, and Alan followed Mom. I followed behind Alan. I usually was the last one following no matter where we went. I heard Mom gasp and start to cry. Then I heard Mike and Bob gasp and start to cry. Then I heard Alan gasp and start to cry. I was getting very scared. Then I saw Dad. My stomach got queasy and I thought I was going to pass out. Dad's entire chest looked like ground up hamburger meat. I started to weep. To this day, I can still see Dad's face. He smiled at me and said, "Don't worry, I'm going to be just fine." I sobbingly said, "I love you." I ran over and hugged Mom. Then the nurse sternly ushered us back to the waiting room.

We waited in the waiting room for over four hours. Finally, the heart specialist came into the waiting room. He told Mom the surgery was successful. The doctor said he had some damage done to the heart but Dad was a strong-willed man. He said they did a skin graft. They took skin from his thigh and grafted it onto his chest. He said Dad was in critical condition and would stay in intensive care for another day or two.

The doctor was not kidding when he said Dad was a strong-willed man. Dad walked out of that hospital five days later. We were so happy to have Dad back home. Mom told us we would have to be on our best behavior. She said Dad would need a lot of rest. Mom said Dad did not need to worry about what his boys were doing. She told us to stay out of mischief. I thought that was an odd thing for Mom to say. I didn't think I ever got into mischief. I was mighty happy Dad was home and recovering from that horrible accident.

CHAPTER 19

The Nickname

It was still chilly the second week in April 1963. It had been six months ago when Dad had his horrible accident. He had not worked since that date. I did not realize what our financial situation was like. I did not realize Dad incurred high medical bills due to the horrible accident. I did not realize Dad had no income for six months.

I did realize that Dad and Mom were constantly arguing and yelling at each other. I did realize there was less food on the table. I learned to eat quickly or my brothers would eat what food was on the table. One morning, I saw Mom take an almost empty quart of milk and fill it halfway with water. There was no more of my favorite cinnamon sugar toast. I noticed we had potato soup more and more often. As the days went on, I noticed the potato soup had less and less potatoes and was more and more soup. Mostly just water.

We had four more weeks of school. We normally packed a lunch sack for school every day. It got to the point where we did not have any bread or lunchmeat to pack a lunch with. So we didn't pack anything. Therefore, we had nothing to eat at school during lunch period.

When I went to the school cafeteria at lunch time, I just sat at a table. On Wednesday, I went to the school cafeteria and sat at a table by myself. A teacher walked up to me and asked, "Aren't you going to eat?" I told the teacher I forgot my lunch bag and left it at the house. The teacher asked, "Did you forget your lunch sack the last two days also?" I didn't reply.

The teacher said, "Go get you a tray of food. I'll pay for it." I stared at her and said sharply, "I'm a Tracey, and I earn my keep." The teacher gave me a bewildered look then said, "Okay, when you are done eating, you can take out the cafeteria trash to the incinerator. That way you will be earning your keep. Now, go get you a tray of food." That made sense to me. I would be earning my keep so I said, "Okay." I walked over to the food line, picked up a tray, and got some food. I even got a slice of bread. I gobbled up that food fast from habit. Like I said, I had three brothers who would eat everything if you let them. That food was delicious.

After I ate, I went to the teacher who offered me my new job of taking out the cafeteria trash. She showed me where the replacement garbage bags were stored. She told me to take two new garbage bags to the trash cans by the two exit doors. She told me to take out the full garbage bags out of the trashcans. She told me to replace them with the new garbage bags. She told me to take the full garbage bags to the incinerator. She told me to place the full garbage bags in a pile on the right side of the incinerator. She told me I could not put the trash in the incinerator. She said only the janitor could put the trash in the incinerator. She asked me if I understood her instructions. I said, "Yes, ma'am." Then I went to work.

I got two new garbage bags from storage. There was one large trash can by each exit. I walked to the farthest exit. I pulled the garbage bag out of the trash can and twisted the top of the bag. I replaced the garbage bag with a new one. I heard a couple of kids giggling as they exited the cafeteria. I carried the trash bag to the other exit and repeated the process. As before, a couple kids exiting this exit door also pointed at me and giggled. I just glared at them. I carried both trash bags out to the incinerator. I felt good about myself. I was a Tracey and I earned my keep.

On Thursday, the next day, I went to the food line with a tray. The cafeteria lady at the start of the line asked me for my lunch money. I told her I earn my lunch by taking out the trash. The kid behind me snickered. The cafeteria lady said she didn't know any-thing about it. She made me leave the food line. I was walking to an empty table when the teacher who gave me my job walked in. She saw me and immediately walked over to the cafeteria lady.

They talked a few minutes and the teacher waved me over to the food line. The teacher handed me a tray and said everything has been taken care of. "You won't have this problem anymore." I did everything like I did yesterday. I ate the good food fast. I pulled the trash bags out of the trash cans. I replaced them with new trash bags. The kids would snicker and giggle. I would take the full trash bags to the incinerator. Again, I felt good about myself. I was a Tracey and I earned my keep.

On Friday, the teacher that gave me my job met me when I walked into the cafeteria. She told me my brother Alan and I would be taking the trash out at the end of the school day. She said we would get out of our last class fifteen minutes early to take out the cafeteria trash. That was just fine with me. I would earn my keep and get out of my last class fifteen minutes early. This was a win/win situation.

On Friday, fifteen minutes before my last class ended, my teacher told me to report to the cafeteria. When I was walking to the cafeteria, I met Alan walking to the cafeteria. Alan said, "I like getting out of my last class fifteen minutes early." We walked into the cafeteria. Alan went into the room where they prepared the cafeteria food. Alan's job was to empty the trash cans in the kitchen area. I emptied the full garbage bags from both trash cans. I replaced the trash cans with new garbage bags just like I did the last two days. Only this time, the cafeteria was empty. There were no kids giggling and pointing fingers at me. There was peace and quiet while I per-formed my chores. I thought, "This is great." I get to get out of my last class fifteen minutes early. There are no kids around to make fun of me. Kids giggling at me when I emptied the trash cans didn't really bother me. After all, I was a Tracey and I earned my keep.

I left the cafeteria with my two large garbage bags full of trash. I met Alan carrying his two large garbage bags full of trash. We walked together to the incinerator dragging our garbage bags behind us. We dumped the garbage bags in a pile on the right side of the incinerator. We were not allowed to put the trash in the incinerator. The teacher told us only the janitor could put the garbage bags in the incinerator.

We were walking to our school bus to take us home. We passed a group of five to six boys. They were all fifth graders. They started chanting, "Trashy Tracey," "Trashy Tracey," "Trashy Tracey." This infuriated Alan. He turned around and hauled ass straight toward the crowd of boys with fists clenched. I knew Alan didn't have a chance with that many fifth graders. So I clenched my fists and hauled ass after Alan. Alan hit the crowd of boys first. I followed into the crowd with my fist swinging. Someone hit me in the left eye. I yelled out in pain but kept swinging. Finally, the crowd of boys had enough and ran off. Alan fared better than I did. He only ended up with a small bruise on his shoulder. I ended up with a black eye. I might have done better if I hadn't closed my eyes when I hit the crowd of boys with my fists swinging.

Monday was the start of a new school week. I would be doing the same thing as I did last week. Only this week, I would be getting out of my last class fifteen minutes early every day. I would be taking out the trash every day. I would earn my keep. I went to the cafeteria at lunch time. I got in line and got a good tasty lunch. When I walked to the table, I heard someone say, "There goes Trashy Tracey," from across the room. I ignored everyone and sat down at a table by myself. I ate my lunch and started daydreaming about being a cowboy in the wild west.

Alan and I took out the cafeteria trash every day. Alan and I worked quietly and did not joke around when completing our chores. I think Alan hated to take out the trash. Even if he was earning his keep. On Friday, we had finished taking out the trash to the incinerator. We were heading to our school bus. I was excited school was out for the weekend. I was in a great mood. I was joking around with Alan. Alan lightened up and started having a little fun. We almost got to the bus. Then we heard chanting, "Trashy Tracey," "Trashy Tracey," "Trashy Tracey." The chanting came from the other side of the school bus. Alan was infuriated again. I was angry because they ruined the end of a good day.

I saw Alan clench his fists. I knew there was no way out of this fight. I clenched my fists. Alan saw me clench my fists and he said, "Let's go beat them to a pulp." We ran around to the other side of the bus. This time there were about a dozen sixth graders waiting for us. I don't know if we were just hard headed or stupid. But instead of stopping, we hauled ass straight toward the crowd just like we did the last time. Only this time, I kept my eyes opened. Alan was skinny. But Alan was a strong skinny kid. And Alan was fast. Alan had hit two of the boys and was about to hit the third boy when I got to the crowd. Since I had my eyes opened this time, I was able to duck and miss a fist headed for my eye. I threw a punch and hit him in the nose. Blood spurted from his nose and he went running away. I was about to punch another boy in the face when I got punched on the side of the head. I fell down. Several boys jumped on top of me hitting me all over. As I was lying on the ground, I kicked a couple boys in the stomach.

The fight only lasted a few minutes. Our cool school bus driver broke up the fight and pulled the few remaining sixth graders off of us. When the fight was all over, I realized I fared better the last time when I closed my eyes and went in swinging. This time, I had two black eyes and bruises on my back, shoulder, and stomach. Alan didn't fare as well this time either. He had one black eye and bruises on his back and shoulders. Alan said, "Well, we went down fighting. I think we put the hurt on about seven or eight of the boys."

Our cool school bus driver looked us over. He asked, "Are you boys okay?" We both said, "Yeah, we're fine." Our cool bus driver asked, "Are you boys crazy? Why in the world would you two boys fight twelve sixth graders?" We told him they called us, "Trashy Tracey." Alan said, "So we thought we would live up to our nickname and trash them." Our school bus driver asked, "Why do they call you Trashy Tracey." I explained, "We take out the cafeteria trash to the incinerator to pay for our lunch." Alan said, "Yeah, we take out the trash." Our cool school bus driver said, "Well, I guess I can't blame you." Then he said, "After this fight, they may nickname you 'Crazy Tracey' for fighting two against twelve. I sure would." I thought about what the cool school bus driver said. I liked the nickname "Crazy Tracey" a lot better than "Trashy Tracey." Then our cool school bus driver looked us over one more time and asked, "Are you sure both of you are okay?" We laughed and told him yes, you can take us home now.

Mom worked nights at the hospital so she didn't notice our black eyes until the next day. She shook her head and asked what happened to us. We had planned to tell her we got beat up playing football. So that is was we told her. It wasn't an entire lie. We did get beat up. Bob, Alan, and I went outside and played cowboys and Indians. We practiced fighting the Indians for quite some time. I needed all the practice I could get.

On Monday, I repeated the same things I did the last week. Only this time, both my eyes were still black and blue. I wasn't in any pain. At lunchtime, I went to the cafeteria and got in the lunch line. I got my lunch that I earned by taking out the trash. I walked to an empty table and sat down. I ate my lunch fast like I always did. Then I finally realized, no one hollered, there goes "Trashy Tracey." When I left the lunch cafeteria, I thought I heard someone murmur, "He's crazy."

The weekdays past. I did not hear one person holler or murmur, "There goes Trashy Tracey." On Friday Alan and I were ready for another crowd of sixth graders to chant "Trashy Tracey." This time Alan and I both picked up a sizable stick by the incinerator. We were going to even the odds when we had our next fight. We walked to the school bus. We got on the school bus. There was no chanting, "Trashy Tracey." There was no crowd of sixth graders. We were all by ourselves on the school bus. It was unusually quiet for a Friday afternoon. I guess our nickname "Trashy Tracey" was short lived.

Our cool school bus driver stepped in the bus. He looked down the aisle. He saw just Alan and I. Our cool school bus driver said, "I guess the 'Crazy Traceys' whipped the sixth graders." We just laughed. Our new nickname "Crazy Tracey" was born. For some reason that nickname "Crazy Tracey" seemed to stay with us for quite a while.

CHAPTER 20

Leaving Kansas

It was September 1963, when everything started to fall apart. It had been almost a year since Dad was unable to work because of his horrible accident. It seemed to me Dad and Mom had been arguing on a daily basis. Sometimes, the arguments got so heated, dishes would be thrown and broken. I soon found out why they were constantly arguing.

Dad said, "We are getting evicted out of our farmhouse." I couldn't believe it. The farmhouse that looked like a shack when we first moved in. The farmhouse, the barn and the storage shed that we fixed up. We had earned our keep. Now the owner was going to evict us. Like I said before, I was realizing life was not very fair. Life is what it is.

Dad told us we were moving to Ohio. It was a Friday morning when Dad drove up with a U-haul trailer. Dad was a no-nonsense type of person. Dad immediately told us to load the furniture onto the trailer. Mike and Bob was in charge of loading their bedroom furniture onto the trailer. Alan and I were responsible for loading our bedroom furniture onto the trailer. We got right to work. Alan and I loaded our mattress onto the trailer. Alan and I packed our clothes into a box. Both our clothes fit into one box. Then Alan and I loaded our dresser onto the trailer. Alan loaded our box of clothes.

I took the picture off the wall. As soon as I took the picture off the wall, I saw that big hole in the sheetrock. I had a flashback of Alan lying on the bed with his legs coiled and shoving me flying into the air. I remembered how my head went right through the sheetrock. I thought, "Uh-oh, I'm in big trouble now." I quickly and quietly hung the picture back on the wall covering the hole in the sheetrock.

It was Friday afternoon when we had everything loaded on the U-haul trailer. Dad walked throughout the house to make sure everything was loaded. He went into Mike and Bob's bedroom. Then he went into Alan and my bedroom. I heard Dad say, "Alan and Jeff, you left a picture hanging on the wall." Dad walked over to the picture and took it off the wall. I heard Dad yell, "What the hell happened here?"

I had learned my lesson about lying. I knew I was not very good at lying. I walked up to Dad and said, "Alan and I were playing. He pushed me in the air and my head landed in the wall." Dad just laughed and said, "Well, we fixed several holes when we moved in the house. We may as well leave a few holes when we move out." Then Dad added, "What are they going to do? Evict us." Then he laughed as he handed me the picture. I was glad I didn't lie as I took the picture to the trailer.

Dad said we will camp out in the house tonight. We will head out at first light in the morning. The first light came quick. I was sound asleep when Dad hollered, "Time to move out." We all sleepily climbed into the car. By 7:00 a.m. Saturday morning, we were on the highway. We were leaving Kansas behind and heading toward Ohio. But this time, we were leaving as a reunited family.

Little did I know, Kansas was the best time of my childhood life. The next chapter of my life brought true meaning to "Life isn't always fair." Life is what it is. Nothing lasts forever and do not rely on anyone but yourself. But one thing was for certain, I earned my keep.

THE END

— ABOUT THE AUTHOR —

Jeffery Tracey was born April 2, 1952, in Mt. Vernon, Ohio. Jeffery moved several times during his childhood. He went to eight different school districts while attending grades one to twelve. He graduated from South Houston High School in 1970 at South Houston, Texas. He attended San Jacinto College concentrating on computer courses.

Jeffery Tracey retired from the U.S. Postal Service after thirty-eight years of service. He started as a letter carrier. He was promoted to supervisor, manager, and postmaster. He was detailed to Headquarters in Washington D.C. as a delivery analyst for a couple years. He provided internal training for delivery supervisors. He assisted in restoring mail delivery service in the aftermath of hurricane Katrina in New Orleans, Louisiana.

After raising a family and dedicating his life to the U.S. Postal Service, he started working on his passion of writing short stories.

CPSIA information can be obtained
at www.ICGtesting.com
Printed in the USA
FFOW05n2335110817

9 781683 489788